# MY
# MEXICAN MESA,
# Y LISTO!

BEAUTIFUL FLAVORS, FAMILY STYLE

# MY MEXICAN MESA,
# Y LISTO!

## JENNY MARTINEZ

with Ann Volkwein
Photography by Jennifer Chong

Simon Element

New York London Toronto Sydney New Delhi

TO MOM AND DAD, BERTHA AND JESUS NEGRETE, for loving me unconditionally and teaching me how to cook so good!

TO MY HUSBAND, ARNULFO, for continuously showing me all his love and making me laugh all the time. MY DAUGHTER, CINDY, God sent you to me as he knew I needed someone like to you take me to this level. Thank you for everything. You have done such a great job handling this new world for you and all of us!

ANTHONY, you taught me how to be a mom. Sorry, I know we had to learn the hard way, but thank you for being such a good son and for always jumping in whenever your family needs you. Thank you and Melissa for giving us the greatest joy of being grandparents for the very first time. Love you, Emilia!

EVAN, oh my Evan . . . always with a smile and extending a helping hand to everyone, you have such a good heart; thank you, mijo.

JOSH, my baby but the one always shocks me with all the dishes you prepare—proving me wrong by making fresh homemade pasta when I dared you! You push all my buttons, but thank you for loving your family the way you do.

An Imprint of Simon & Schuster, LLC
1230 Avenue of the Americas
New York, NY 10020

Copyright © 2024 by Juana Martinez

Photography copyright © 2024 by Jennifer Chong

All rights reserved, including the right to reproduce this book or portions thereof in any form whatsoever. For information, address Simon Element Subsidiary Rights Department, 1230 Avenue of the Americas, New York, NY 10020.

First Simon Element hardcover edition April 2024

SIMON ELEMENT is a trademark of Simon & Schuster, LLC

Simon & Schuster: Celebrating 100 Years of Publishing Since 1924

For information about special discounts for bulk purchases, please contact Simon & Schuster Special Sales at 1-866-506-1949 or business@simonandschuster.com.

The Simon & Schuster Speakers Bureau can bring authors to your live event. For more information or to book an event, contact the Simon & Schuster Speakers Bureau at 1-866-248-3049 or visit our website at www.simonspeakers.com.

Food Stylist: Laura Kinsey Dolph

Props Stylist: Stephanie Hanes

Photo Assistant: David K. Peng

Food Stylist 1st Assistant: Danielle Marin

Food Stylist 2nd Assistant: Courtney Weis, Bee Berrie, and Elle Debell

Prop Stylist Assistant: Alixandra Macmillan-Fiedel

Interior & cover design by Jen Wang

Manufactured in China

10 9 8 7 6 5 4 3 2 1

Library of Congress Cataloging-in-Publication Data has been applied for.

ISBN 978-1-6680-0997-0

ISBN 978-1-6680-0996-3 (ebook)

# CONTENTS

✦

# APPETIZERS

**39**
**Spicy Habanero Guacamole**

**40**
**Mexican Queso**
(CHEESE DIP)

**43**
**Mexican Bolillos**

**45**
**Papas Rellenas**
(STUFFED BAKED POTATOES)

**46**
**Guasanas**
(FRESH GREEN GARBANZOS)

**49**
**Papitas Enchiladas**
(SMALL WAX POTATOES IN CHILE SAUCE)

**52**
**Pulpo a las Brazas**
(GRILLED OCTOPUS WITH CITRUS GARLIC BUTTER)

✦

# TACOS, TAQUITOS & TAMALES

**57**
**Quesabirria Tacos**

**58**
**Tacos de Camaron, Baja Style**
(BATTERED SHRIMP TACOS)

**60**
**Tacos de Canasta–Carne Deshebrada, Papa con Chorizo, y Frijoles**
(3 BASKET-STYLE TACOS)

**62**
**Tacos de Alambre**
(MEATY STRINGY CHEESE TACOS)

**63**
**Tacos de Lengua**
(BEEF TONGUE TACOS)

**64**
**Tacos de Tripas**
(BEEF INTESTINE TACOS)

**67**
**Taquitos de Papa**
(FRIED POTATO TAQUITOS)

**70**
**Taquitos de Carne con Chipotle y Queso Oaxaca**
(BEEF TAQUITOS WITH CHIPOTLE AND CHEESE)

**74**
**Tamales de Puerco en Chile Rojo**
(RED CHILI PORK TAMALES)

**76**
**Tamales de Pollo Salsa Verde**
(GREEN SALSA CHICKEN TAMALES)

**78**
**Tamales de 3 Rajas**
(3-PEPPER CHEESE TAMALES)

**80**
**Tamales de Elote**
(SWEET CORN TAMALES)

# CHICKEN, FISH & VEGETARIAN

85
**Habanero
Chicken Wings**

86
**Chicken Tinga**
(SHREDDED CHICKEN
WITH CHIPOTLE SAUCE)

89
**Enchiladas de Pollo
en Salsa Verde**
(GREEN CHICKEN ENCHILADAS)

91
**Mole Rojo
Pollo Estilo Nayarit**
(RED MOLE CHICKEN, NAYARIT
STYLE)

94
**Mole Negro de Pollo**
(BLACK MOLE CHICKEN)

96
**Camarones a la Diabla**
(DEVIL'S SHRIMP)

99
**Pescado
Zarandeado Estilo
Nayarit**
(MEXICAN GRILLED
RED SNAPPER)

100
**Salmon con
Salsa de Mango**
(GRILLED SALMON
WITH MANGO SALSA)

104
**Mexican Quesadillas, Michoacan Style**
(POTATO, GREEN PEPPER, AND BEANS-STUFFED TORTILLA DOUGH)

# PORK & BEEF

109
**Carnitas**
(SLOW COOKED FRIED PORK)

110
**Manchamantel**
(FRIED PORK IN
DARK CHILI SAUCE)

112
**Costillitas en Salsa Verde**
(PORK SHORT RIBS IN
GREEN SAUCE)

114
**Gorditas de Queso
con Chorizo**
(CHEESE AND CHORIZO FRIED
TORTILLAS)

116
**Chiles en Nogada**
(BEEF-STUFFED POBLANOS IN
WALNUT SAUCE)

120
**Tostadas de Deshebrada**
(SHREDDED BEEF TOSTADAS)

123
**Bistec Ranchero**
(RANCHERO BEEF SKIRT STEAK)

125
**Enchiladas de Carne
Molida en Chile Rojo**
(RED CHILE BEEF ENCHILADAS)

# STEWS & SOUPS

**130**
**Birria de Res**
(MEXICAN BEEF STEW)

**134**
**Carne en Su Jugo**
(BEEF COOKED
IN ITS OWN JUICES)

**137**
**Caldo de
Albóndigas**
(MEXICAN
MEATBALL SOUP)

**141**
**Pozole Verde**
(GREEN PORK AND
CHICKEN STEW)

**142**
**Caldo de Res**
(BEEF AND
VEGETABLE SOUP)

# RICE & BEANS

**146**
**Arroz Rojo**
(MEXICAN RED RICE)

**149**
**Cilantro Lime Rice**

**150**
**Arroz Verde Poblano
con Queso**
(GREEN POBLANO CHEESE RICE)

**153**
**Frijoles Charros**
(CHARRO BEANS)

**154**
**Frijoles Puercos**
(PORK BEANS)

**157**
**Frijoles Fritos**
(REFRIED BEANS)

**158**
**Old-Fashioned Pinto Beans**

# TORTILLAS, SALSAS & MORE

**162**
**Homemade
Flour Tortillas**

**166**
**Homemade Corn Tortillas**

**167**
**Chorizo Flour Tortillas**

**168**
**Salsa con Queso**
(SALSA WITH CHEESY CHUNKS)

**170**
**Salsa Taquera**
(TACO STAND SALSA)

**173**
**Salsa Cruda**
(RAW SALSA)

**174**
**Chile de Aceite**
(CHILI OIL)

**177**
**Salsa Tatemada
de Molcajete**

**178**
**Ahumada Salsa Morita**
(SMOKY MORITA SALSA)

**179**
**Dad's Tomatillo Salsa**

**180**
**Mom's Tomato Sauce**

# DESERTS

# DRINKS

# ✦ ✦ ✦
# INTRODUCTION

When I think about my love for food and cooking, it's easy to see how food and its ties to family and friends has shaped my life. Food is the connective force, always gathering us around the table. My dad first started his business in Mexico selling oysters and coctel de camarones (shrimp cocktail) from a street stand. It was from his cart, while opening an oyster, that he spotted my mother. She was in Chapala Jalisco, one and a half hours away from her hometown of Michoacan, to help her sister with her first child. She was very reluctant to have a boyfriend who lived so far from home, however handsome or successful. He chased her for two years before she agreed to date him. She says it was like a Cinderella story, as she was very poor, and when they were married, she suddenly went from having no shoes to helping her husband run a business. They eventually bought a corner store and lived next door. My dad was constantly feeding little neighborhood kids who had no money, calling it "even" when they'd help him around the store. He was happy serving people, hungry people. He's humble, with a lifetime of friends as a result. And to this day, you can see he's still madly in love with my mother, and he still loves serving people. Even at *my* house, he'll come over and start cooking or taking care of us; I have to tell him to sit down! Relax! But he never seems to become tired, and I've never seen him angry.

My mother began cooking for her family at the age of eight. She learned to make dough, stoke the wood fire she cooked over, and feed her younger siblings (she was the oldest of eighteen). I have five sisters and one brother, all of us born in Mexico, and she always taught us that we must know how to cook, in case of an emergency—and that love starts growing through the belly. I took to cooking from the start. My mom always made sure we knew the basics, and we were surrounded by her food, the aromas, and visuals. We'd wake up to the smell of her birria all through the house on the morning of a wedding, with all my cousins piled in, thirty people under one roof! (Mexicans don't believe in staying in hotels.) I was married at age seventeen, and my husband's mother and his visiting aunts and uncles were impressed that I was able to cook at such a young age. A woman who can cook is valued in

Mexican culture! I'd call my mother for tips, and somehow figure out how to make things without any precise measurements ever being shared. But I had the palate and I'd watched my mother all those years. I have always been curious, I joke that I am a "chismosa," but in a good way. I'll ask one hundred questions when I am interested in something someone is cooking. I am nosy about ingredients and techniques. And if they don't want to share, that's OK. If you don't ask, you will never know. I love to smell my food before I take a bite. People notice that and ask me what I am doing. But, with the rare exception, like coffee, you can tell what something is going to taste like from the smell alone. I can tell what's in it and if I am going to like it 95 percent of the time.

My husband loves everything I cook for him, and when he comes home, he says, OMG it smells so good! He thanks me for every meal. He says he doesn't cook, he just "stirs the pot and moves the spoon." In reality, he's the king of the barbecue, and we live and cook outside from sun up to sun down all summer. Being in front of the fire and achieving the perfect grilling temperatures is no joke, and it takes technique that I just don't have. He will forever be my backbone.

I have been blessed with my entire family, as every day they are grateful for the meals I serve. And I am proud to say, each of my four kids can find their way around the kitchen. They've all surpassed my expectations. Cindy is my baker and does everything from scratch, from cinnamon rolls to carrot cake. She even learned how to make flour tortillas before I did! She's got the patience, and I am always in a hurry. She'll say, "No, Mom, put a little love into the dough, just massage it." While I'm thinking, there is no time for massages! But she also understands the science behind food and is a perfectionist. Her pastries are better than the bakery's. My oldest son, Anthony, is an artist in the kitchen. He takes his time and tells me, "let me do my thing!" It always comes out delicious and gorgeous, whether it's sushi, an omelet, or a creative cocktail. I call him my personal mixologist. I call my third child, Evan, my Keto child. He struggled with weight at one point, so he got himself on a regimen, stuck to it, and lost thirty pounds— at age twelve! It was a huge transformation that took so much discipline. He will come into the kitchen and whip up a smoothie or grab some fresh fruit or vegetables for himself. He gets it done, his way. Josh, my baby, is the most rabid one in the kitchen. (In fact, he's wild in many ways.) At age ten he told me he wanted to learn how to cook. I said he was too young, but he insisted that he could do it. Well, he always shocks me. Last year, we were sent a pasta maker, and he decided he was going to make fresh pasta. This is something I had never done before, and I told him it was too hard. But he persisted, and lo and behold, we were soon sitting around with bowls of fresh pasta cooked up by a twelve-year-old. He challenges me, but he achieves his goals—and he gives me gray hair.

Of course, my cooking has improved since I was a young wife, and even now, I see the beauty in every recipe. I don't have a favorite because I love food in general. This is where my catch phrase "BEAUTIFUL!" got its whole tone. It's my heart, and I think people can feel that when I say it. When my daughter first suggested that I do food on TikTok, she encouraged me to be myself, saying, just do what you do and bring your energy to it. It was the beginning of the pandemic and the last thing I wanted was another app on my phone. But she got me going. It was her idea to do the birria recipe, and I happened to have all the ingredients on hand. We posted the video at 7 p.m. and by 7 a.m. the next morning my phone was blowing up, it had gone viral and we'd had 1 million views. It was crazy, and as we continued to post, the followers kept growing. There were days we had 40,000 new followers, and in a couple of months we had over 1 million. I began to doubt that TikTok was real and that the fans were real people. But the stories would come in, from young and old. I was bringing back memories of childhood, sharing recipes that they remembered their grandmothers cooking. I was just making simple, traditional, Mexican meals and trying to make them easy to understand, not perfect. I wanted people to fall in love with cooking.

It wasn't long before we had our first major collaboration with a brand, Bounty, and Gordon Ramsay. Food Network appearances and a Triple G (*Guy's Grocery Games*) win followed. We didn't know what we were doing at first, looking at all the contracts and negotiating, but between my very smart daughter and me, we've been able to navigate. This book is my opportunity to share my recipes in full (with measurements!) with my fans, and to honor my family. We are a team, my husband and kids back me up in whatever I do, and we all do that for one another. The kitchen is the heart of the home. When we bought our house years ago, we had a huge master bedroom and a tiny kitchen, so we took half the bedroom and expanded the kitchen space. It's where we live, and where we choose to be together as a family. My kids still hang out in that kitchen, and the oldest one is thirty! They say you're a rich man if your children choose to hang out with you, and this is still a family affair. But it extends beyond family, and when we have people over, they often lose track of time. It's all about great food, good conversation—and the occasional karaoke.

I am so happy to be able to pass these recipes down to my fans, my family, and this next generation. I hope they bring back memories for some, and spark interest for others. And most of all, I hope these recipes are cooked with love, because if they are, just watch, they will come out amazing.

# BEAUTiFULLLL!!! Y Listo!

# BREAKFAST & LUNCH

## Chilaquiles Divorciados
(DIVORCED CHILAQUILES)

✦

## Mexican Omelet

✦

## Huevos a Caballo
(EGGS ON HORSEBACK)

✦

## Coctel de Camaron
(DAD'S FAMOUS SHRIMP COCKTAIL)

✦

## Aguachile Verde
(SHRIMP IN GREEN "CHILE WATER")

✦

## Dad's Ceviche de Pescado
(FISH CEVICHE)

✦

## Sopita de Fideo
(FIDEO SOUP)

✦

## Poblano Pasta Verde
(ROASTED CHILE GREEN PASTA)

✦

## Creamy Chipotle Pasta

✦

## Mexican Wedding Macaroni Salad

✦

## Chile Rellenos
(BATTERED PEPPERS STUFFED WITH CHEESE)

✦

## Mexican Buffalo Chicken Burrito

✦

## Chile Con Carne
(MEXICAN BEEF CHILI)

✦

## Esquite
(MEXICAN CORN IN A CUP)

✦

# CHILAQUILES DIVORCIADOS

DIVORCED CHILAQUILES

DIVORCED CHILAQUILES

Prep time: 30 minutes
Cook time: 45 minutes
SERVES 6 TO 8

2½ cups plus 1 tablespoon canola oil, divided

24 (6-inch) corn tortillas, cut into 1-inch squares

8 large eggs

¼ white onion, diced

4 ounces queso fresco, crumbled

**For the Green Salsa**

6 green tomatillos

2 fresh jalapeño chiles

1 bunch fresh cilantro

¼ white onion

2 garlic cloves

2 tablespoons chicken bouillon powder

**For the Red Salsa**

2 Roma tomatoes

2 dried guajillo chiles

2 dried puya chiles

2 dried chiles de árbol

¼ white onion

2 garlic cloves

2 tablespoons chicken bouillon powder

I am the type who always wants ALL the salsas. So, when I saw this version at a restaurant, which features one dish divided ("divorced") by half roja and half verde salsas, I was in. This is a weekend breakfast recipe the family gets excited to have together. There are many ways to eat it, but I like mine topped off with an egg. Many people make the mistake of serving the salsa on top of the tortillas, but the authentic way to make chilaquiles is to simmer the tortilla chips briefly in the salsa. You want them to absorb some salsa but not too much as you want them to remain a bit crispy.

1 • In a medium pan, heat 2 cups of oil over medium heat. Check the heat by dipping a wooden spoon into the hot oil; if it sizzles, you're ready. Fry the tortilla squares in batches, stirring frequently, until crispy and golden brown (like tortilla chips), 5 to 7 minutes. Set aside in a tray lined with paper towels in a single layer to drain.

2 • Make the green salsa: In a small saucepan, bring 2 cups of water to a boil over medium-high heat. Add the tomatillos and jalapeños and cook until softened, about 5 minutes. Do not let the tomatillos burst; cook just until they start to brown then remove the pan from the heat, or they will become bitter. Do not drain. Transfer the mixture to a blender. Add the cilantro, onion, garlic, and chicken bouillon powder and blend until smooth. Pour into a bowl and set aside.

(recipe continues)

3 • Make the red salsa: In a separate small saucepan, bring 2 cups of water to a boil over medium-high heat. Add the tomatoes, guajillos, puyas, and chiles de árbol. Boil until softened, about 8 minutes. Do not drain. Transfer the mixture to a blender. Add the onion, garlic, and chicken bouillon powder and blend until smooth. Set aside.

4 • In a medium skillet, heat 2 tablespoons of oil over medium-low heat. Add 2 eggs, cover, and cook, until medium done, about 3 minutes or to your preference. Repeat with the remaining eggs. Set aside.

5 • In a large cast-iron skillet, heat the remaining 1 tablespoon of oil over medium heat. Add the diced onion and cook, stirring frequently, until the oil is flavored, about 2 minutes. Add the tortilla chips and stir to warm through, about 1 minute. Drizzle the green salsa over one half of the chips and drizzle the red salsa on the other half. Gently stir the salsas in, keeping them separate, simmer for 5 minutes, then sprinkle the queso fresco on top, and top with the over-easy eggs. Drizzle more salsa on top of the eggs, if desired. Remove the pan from the heat. Serve straight out of the skillet.

Y LISTO AND ENJOY!

# MEXiCAN OMELET

Prep time: 30 minutes
Cook time: 10 minutes
SERVES 4 TO 6

10 large eggs

3 teaspoons whole milk

1 teaspoon salt

1 teaspoon freshly ground black pepper

1 (1-pound) link longaniza (spicy pork sausage), casing removed

3 Roma tomatoes, diced

½ white onion, diced

1 bunch fresh cilantro, chopped

1 fresh serrano chile, diced

1 stick (8 tablespoons) unsalted butter, divided

3 cups shredded Mexican blend cheese

## Toppings

2 avocados, pitted, peeled, and sliced

½ cup sour cream

½ cup red salsa (see page 7)

½ bunch fresh cilantro, chopped

My oldest son, Anthony, is literally the best at making omelets. I suck at it! But I still make them, just not as pretty and perfectly as he does. Whenever he cooks, he makes beautiful dishes. It's like art for him. Here, I am using Anthony's technique for my favorite omelet. It uses longaniza, which is very similar to chorizo but with more spices. It's a bit more meaty than chorizo as well, so it stays in larger chunks after it's cooked, which I prefer. I give full credit to Anthony for a simple omelet because it's harder than it looks. There are so many ways to mess it up; burning it or having it fall apart. Make sure that you do not have the heat too high and always wipe the pan clean between omelets. That's his secret. BEAUTI-FULLL!!!

When I am cooking, I want to get it done and I am usually less patient, but here it's a necessity. We fill it with a picadillo-style combination of veggies—red, white, and green, just like the Mexican flag.

1 • Crack the eggs into a medium bowl, add the milk, salt, and pepper, whisk, and set aside.

2 • In a medium skillet, cook the longaniza over medium heat, stirring frequently and breaking it up with a spoon, until crumbled and browned, 5 to 7 minutes. Set aside.

3 • In a medium bowl, mix the tomatoes, onion, cilantro, and serrano.

4 • In a small pan, melt 1 tablespoon of butter over medium-low heat. Add 2 tablespoons of the vegetable mixture and cook, stirring, until tender but not mushy, about 3 minutes. Add ½ cup of the egg mixture and tilt the pan until the eggs fully covers the bottom. Once the eggs are halfway cooked, about 2 minutes, add ¼ cup of shredded cheese on one half of the eggs, then fold the other side over the cheese to form your omelet. Allow the eggs to fully cook and the cheese to melt, about 2 more minutes. Transfer to a serving plate and top off with avocado slices, sour cream, salsa, and cilantro. Repeat to make the remaining omelets.

Y LISTO AND ENJOY!

# EGGS ON HORSEBACK

# HUEVOS A CABALLO

Prep time: 10 minutes
Cook time: 35 minutes

SERVES 6

1 cup plus 6 tablespoons canola oil, divided

1½ white onions, thinly sliced

12 (6-inch) corn tortillas

3 tablespoons Mesa Mia; Jenny's Favorite Seasoning

12 large eggs

2 cups Refried Beans (page 157), warmed

## Toppings

1 (8-ounce) package queso fresco, crumbled

1 cup Salsa Tatemada de Molcajete (page 177)

½ cup sour cream

2 avocados, pitted, peeled, and sliced

½ bunch fresh cilantro, chopped

I stole this recipe from my older sister, Tita, who would make it for her husband. It was only when I started seeing it in books or videos that I learned the name of the recipe. She may have caught a segment on a morning show and learned about them that way as well. We lost her to breast cancer four years ago. She loved being in the kitchen and although she didn't have a lot of money, she enjoyed being creative.

These are similar to huevos rancheros, but here the salsa, fried tortilla, and egg are made separately, and the beans are put on the tostada. Then you garnish with fresh onions and salsa roja. As with a lot of Mexican recipes, the ingredients may be similar, but the method makes it taste completely different.

1 • In a medium skillet, heat 3 tablespoons of oil over medium heat. Add the onions and cook, stirring constantly, until lightly browned, 7 to 8 minutes. Set aside.

2 • Prepare a deep bowl lined with paper towels. In a separate, deep skillet, heat 1 cup of oil over medium heat. Check the heat by dipping a wooden spoon into the hot oil; if it sizzles, you're ready. Add a tortilla and fry until golden brown (or until it turns into a crispy tostada!), about 2 minutes on each side. Drain the tortilla and set aside in the prepared bowl. Immediately sprinkle with some of the seasoning while the tostada is still warm. Repeat with the remaining tortillas.

3 • In a separate small skillet, heat the remaining 3 tablespoons of oil over medium-low heat. Add the eggs one at a time and cook sunny side up or as preferred (we make them to order for the family).

4 • To build your Huevos a Caballo, spread 2 to 3 tablespoons of beans on a tostada, place a cooked egg on top of the beans, and top it off with some onions. Add your toppings: sprinkled queso fresco, Salsa Tatemada, a dollop of sour cream, 2 slices of avocado, and a little cilantro.

Y LISTO AND ENJOY!

# DAD'S FAMOUS SHRIMP COCKTAIL

# COCTEL DE CAMARON

Prep time: 1 hour 20 minutes

Cook time: 3 minutes

SERVES 10 TO 12

1¼ white onions, divided

5 Roma tomatoes, divided

1 whole garlic head, equator cut, exposing the raw garlic

4 dried bay leaves

2 tablespoons salt

4 pounds (41/50 count) shrimp, deveined and unpeeled

2 cucumbers

1 bunch fresh cilantro

2 avocados

¾ cup ketchup, divided

¼ cup granulated sugar, divided

## Toppings

4 limes, cut into wedges (optional)

Tapatio hot sauce (optional)

Tostadas or Saltine crackers

This is my dad's famous recipe. At the age of eighteen, he began with an oyster stand, selling them as appetizers, then he upgraded to shrimp cocktails. He built his early married life in Mexico using this recipe. Working that little stand, he kept saving money until he bought an abarrotes, which is a mini market or corner store. My parents built their house from scratch, with the market right next to it, where he also sold sweet bread, Coke—a little bit of everything.

The Mexican recipe is very different from an American shrimp cocktail. To this day, his is the best we have had. My dad is over eighty years old, and when he comes to visit my kids ask, can my abuelito fix it for me? Even though I do it the same way. He says his secret ingredient is the dirt from his fingers. He taste tests it about ten times as he goes, to make sure the ingredients reach the ideal levels. The lime juice or hot sauce amounts are very specific. For him, it's a science.

1 • In a large, tall pot, bring 3 quarts of water to a boil over medium-high heat. Add the ¼ onion, 1 tomato with 2 slits cut on one end, the garlic, bay leaves, and salt. Boil until the vegetables are cooked, about 30 minutes. Add the shrimp and boil until just cooked through, about 3 minutes; do not to overcook. Quickly remove the shrimp from the pot and spread out on a sheet pan to cool. Reserve the shrimp broth.

2 • While the shrimp cools down, prepare the remaining vegetables, placing each in their own individual bowl, so that people can choose their own toppings: Dice the remaining onion and tomato. Peel and dice the cucumbers. Roughly chop the cilantro. Pit, peel, and dice the avocados. At this point, the shrimp should be cool enough to peel. Peel and set aside.

3 • In a large, tall glass (we use very large martini or margarita glasses), put 8 to 12 peeled shrimp with 1 cup of the reserved broth. Add your choice of the diced vegetables and fresh cilantro. Add 1 tablespoon of ketchup and 1 teaspoon of sugar and stir well until the ketchup is thoroughly incorporated. Finish off with lime juice and hot sauce, if desired. Serve with tostadas or crackers.

Y LISTO AND ENJOY!

# SHRIMP IN GREEN "CHILE WATER"

# AGUACHILE VERDE

Prep time: 1 hour
Cook time: 1 hour

SERVES 6 TO 8

2 pounds (26/30 count) shrimp, peeled and deveined

2 cups fresh lime juice, divided

1 tablespoon freshly ground black pepper

1 teaspoon salt

2 bunches fresh cilantro, divided (see Cook's Note)

½ white onion

6 fresh serrano chiles

4 garlic cloves

2 tablespoons chicken bouillon powder

2 cucumbers, peeled, seeded, and half-moon sliced

1 red onion, thinly sliced

1 cup mayonnaise (I use Best Foods or Hellman's), divided

16 (6-inch) corn tostadas

Tapatio hot sauce (optional)

We learned this recipe from my brother, Chuy, who, if he could, would have a diet exclusively of seafood. It's similar to a Mexican shrimp cocktail, but more like a ceviche, as the salsa verde marinates and "cooks" the raw shrimp in its acid. A lot of lime juice is necessary, so we sometimes use a hand press for all the lime squeezing. My preference is to marinate the shrimp for at least an hour. Some people like it less cooked, more raw, but this is the way we enjoy it and it's safer to eat, as well.

## COOK'S NOTE

When making the sauce, use the whole bunch of cilantro, including the stems, because that's where the flavor lives.

1 • Slice each shrimp in half lengthwise. Spread out on a large platter, pour 1 cup of lime juice over the top, and season with the pepper and salt. Marinate in the refrigerator for 1 hour (or for less time if you prefer it on the raw side).

2 • While the shrimp is marinating, prepare the green sauce. In a blender, add the remaining 1 cup of lime juice, 1 bunch of cilantro, the white onion, serranos, garlic, and chicken bouillon powder. Blend until smooth.

3 • After draining the shrimp from the lime juice, pour the green sauce over the shrimp. Top with the cucumbers, red onions, and cilantro sprigs from the remaining bunch. To eat, spread ½ tablespoon of mayonnaise on a tostada and top off with a large spoonful of shrimp aguachile. Drizzle with hot sauce, if desired. Repeat with the remaining tostadas.

Y LISTO AND ENJOY!

# DAD'S CEVICHE DE PESCADO⊙

Prep time: 1 hour 25 minutes
Cook time: 6 hours
**SERVES 10 TO 12**

By the late 1970s we had grown to a family of six in LA. Dad was making $3 an hour, as was my mother, so to make ends meet we would go to parks and sell tostadas de ceviche. They sold like hotcakes. In Ford Park in Bell Gardens, my dad got creative. People would go there to play soccer, and these guys would come off the field and satisfy their hunger with our ceviche. My dad made it his business to know their schedule, and we'd follow the same teams from game to game, park to park. This way, he had a following who didn't need to be introduced to his offerings every time. He would sell out. They would call out to him, "Negrete, bring the tostada!"

I guess I have always been in sales, forever a hustler. Sometimes people would take advantage and not pay. Week after week, I would go after them until they did—

it's money! I didn't understand why my dad kept giving them food if they hadn't paid him for something they'd eaten two months ago. But he's such a good-hearted person, it's hard for him to say no. I always tell him, you are going to go to heaven with shoes and all. It's true. When he had the store back in Mexico there were kids around that didn't have money. He would give them little jobs when he needed the help and would pay them with food. They'd say, "Don Chuy, Don Chuy, what can I help you with?" I was a baby then, but I hear the stories from my older siblings and uncles. And every time we go to Mexico there are people who come running out to greet him, saying thank you, thank you for giving them food and not letting them go hungry. There were so many kids he probably fed, now in their late forties or fifties.

(recipe continues)

6 pounds skinless red
snapper fillets

Juice of 12 fresh limes,
divided

6 Roma tomatoes, diced

2 white onions, diced

1 bunch fresh cilantro,
roughly chopped

1 teaspoon dried oregano

2 tablespoons salt

1 tablespoon freshly
ground black pepper

20 (6-inch) corn tostadas

## Toppings

Mayonnaise (optional)

2 fresh serrano chiles,
thinly sliced into
rounds (optional)

2 avocados, pitted,
peeled, and sliced

Tapatio hot sauce
(optional)

1 • Wash and pat dry the fish fillets. Dice the fish into small pieces; be careful not to make them too small, however, or they will become mushy. Spread the fish out on a sheet pan and pour half of the lime juice over them. Marinate the fish in the refrigerator for 4 to 6 hours; the timing will depend on how fully cooked (in the acid of the lime juice) you prefer the fish. Once the fish is cooked to your liking, grab handfuls of it and gently squeeze out the lime juice. Transfer the drained fish to a large bowl and separate the pieces using your hands. Add the remaining lime juice, the tomatoes, onions, cilantro, oregano, salt, and pepper. Mix well.

2 • To prepare the tostadas, lightly spread 1 teaspoon of mayonnaise, if desired, on each tostada, then add 3 tablespoons of the ceviche, and top with fresh serranos, if desired. Add avocado slices and, if desired, a drizzle of hot sauce.

Y LISTO AND ENJOY!

# SOPiTA DE FIDEO

Prep time: 5 minutes
Cook time: 15 minutes
SERVES 8 TO 10

3 Roma tomatoes

2 Mexican green onions, or 4 regular green onions (see Cook's Note)

2 garlic cloves

2 tablespoons chicken bouillon powder

3 tablespoons canola oil

2 (8-ounce) packages of fideo pasta

¼ white onion, diced

**Toppings** (see Cook's Note)

Queso fresco

Fresh cilantro, roughly chopped

Tapatio hot sauce (optional)

If you were to talk to any Mexican mom, fideo is one of the go-to meals for their babies once they start eating solids at six months. It's so tiny they don't have to chew much. "Stop the Gerber stuff," my mom would say. "Make a sopa de fideo!" My kids would have it at least twice a week, and she would make this for my kids when I was at work. My husband says it's perfect cold weather comfort food that takes you back to childhood. It's a blank canvas on which you can get creative.

The big difference in the way I make fideo versus others is my use of fresh ingredients. Most people use canned tomatoes, but using fresh is a game changer, like when you make your own fresh tomato sauce versus canned. But canned is an option; with Covid that's all I had, and I would make this with tomato paste and sauce, but it does taste different.

1 • In a blender, add 2 cups of water, the tomatoes, green onions, garlic, and chicken bouillon powder. Blend until smooth and set the tomato sauce aside. (Always have the sauce ready before the pasta is done.)

2 • Heat the oil in a medium pan over medium-low heat, add the pasta, and cook, stirring continually, until lightly browned, about 5 minutes.

3 • Add the white onion and cook, stirring, for 1 minute. Add the tomato sauce and cook, stirring, for 1 minute. Add 6 cups of water, increase the heat to medium-high, and bring to a boil . . . BEAUTIFUL! Boil until the pasta is cooked and the broth has slightly reduced, about 10 minutes. Serve in a bowl topped with the queso fresco, a sprinkle of cilantro, and, if desired, a couple drops of hot sauce.

Y LISTO AND ENJOY!

## COOK'S NOTES

Mexican green onions are more mature scallions. The white bulbs are larger and fully formed.

Another serving option is to top the bowl with freshly cooked beans, queso fresco, onion, and chopped tomatoes. And sometimes I don't use any toppings and simply serve the soup with cheese quesadillas or crackers on the side.

## ROASTED CHILE GREEN PASTA
# POBLANO PASTA VERDE

Prep time: 30 minutes
Cook time: 45 minutes
SERVES 8 TO 10

In poblano pepper season Mexican families are poblano crazy. We serve this as a side or main dish. The green color really pops on the pasta, and you don't need to serve meat with it, as it's great to eat it alone. The Oaxacan cheese is wonderful. The poblano is named after the Mexican state of Puebla, but in northern Mexico and the US sometimes you'll find this pepper called pasilla in the stores. But beware that the word "pasilla" can also refer to hatch chiles, which are lighter green, skinny, and long. You can substitute with those, if need be, in this recipe.

1 (16-ounce) package spaghetti

6 fresh poblano chiles

1 white onion, divided

1 cup whole milk

1 bunch fresh cilantro

2 fresh jalapeño chiles

2 tablespoons cream cheese

2 tablespoons chicken bouillon powder

2 tablespoons sour cream

2 garlic cloves, divided

2 tablespoons unsalted butter

3 cups shredded Oaxacan cheese, divided

1 • Preheat the oven to 375°F.

2 • Bring a large pot of water to a boil over medium-high heat and boil the spaghetti per package directions. Reserve 1 cup of the pasta water. Drain the pasta and set aside.

3 • In the meantime, heat a large comal or skillet over medium-high heat, add the poblanos and cook, turning occasionally, until they are charred on all sides, about 6 minutes. (Alternatively, char the poblanos on the stovetop directly over a low open flame.) Put all of the poblano peppers each in gallon-size, resealable plastic bags, and allow to sweat for 10 minutes to help loosen the skin. Peel away the charred layer of skin. Slice each poblano vertically, just enough to remove the seeds. Slice 3 poblanos into strips, or rajas, and leave 3 seeded and skinned but whole and unsliced.

4 • For the sauce: In a blender, add one quarter of the onion, the reserved 1 cup pasta water, the 3 whole poblanos, the milk, cilantro, jalapeños, cream cheese, chicken bouillon powder, sour cream, and 1 garlic clove. Blend until smooth and set aside.

5 • Mince the remaining garlic clove and dice the remaining onion. In a large saucepan over medium heat, melt the butter. Add the garlic and onion and cook, stirring continuously, until the onion is translucent, 3 to 5 minutes. Add the green sauce and

pasta along with 2 cups of Oaxacan cheese and the poblanos strips and mix until blended.

6 • Transfer to a medium 9 x 11-inch baking dish. Bake for 15 to 20 minutes, or until browned on the top. Serve topped with the remaining 1 cup of Oaxacan cheese.

Y LISTO AND ENJOY!

# CREAMY CHIPOTLE PASTA

Prep time: 15 minutes
Cook time: 25 minutes
SERVES 8 TO 10

3 Roma tomatoes, divided

1 white onion, quartered, divided

4 garlic cloves, divided

1 tablespoon salt

1 (16-ounce) package spaghetti

1 (7-ounce) can chipotle peppers in adobo

2 tablespoons mayonnaise

2 tablespoons chicken bouillon powder

1 tablespoon unsalted butter

2 tablespoons sour cream

1 cup grated Cotija cheese

Big Mexican gatherings are often catered potluck style, and people are asked to make the recipes that they're known to "nail." One of the crowd favorites is this pasta. My mom says it fills people up, and if you don't feed them starchy foods like this or potato salad or tortillas, then the carne asada just flies—they'd eat three pounds of meat each otherwise!

Chipotle and poblano peppers are loved by Mexican families. When I post recipes with them, they go crazy, and I do, too. Depending on the chipotle harvest that year, the sauce will vary in sweetness or heat level. So be careful, and taste test, as the spice levels vary from can to can. It's the same thing with chiles de árbol or when using poblanos to make rellenos, they can be fire or not that hot at all. In Mexican kitchens, cans of chipotle peppers are staples. You can make chipotle chicken, or a pasta, or an aioli to put on a fish taco. It's a flexible, smoky hot flavor that you can pretty much spread on everything.

1 • Bring a large pot of water to a boil over medium-high heat. Add 1 tomato, ¼ onion, 1 garlic clove, and the salt. Boil until the water is flavored, about 10 minutes. Add the pasta and cook per package directions. Drain the pasta, reserving ½ cup of pasta water and all of the boiled vegetables. Discard the remaining water.

2 • While the pasta is cooking, in a medium comal or skillet over medium heat, roast the remaining tomatoes, the remaining onion, and remaining garlic, being sure to turn each vegetable to char on all sides, about 3 minutes on each side. Add the tomatoes, onion, and garlic to a blender along with the chipotle peppers in adobo, the mayonnaise, chicken bouillon powder, the reserved ½ cup of pasta water, and the reserved boiled vegetables. Blend until smooth.

3 • In a separate large pot, over medium-low heat, melt the butter, then stir in the pasta and the chipotle sauce; mix until the pasta is fully coated. Stir in the sour cream to make it nice and creamy. Turn off the heat and allow the pasta sit for 5 minutes in order to absorb the chipotle sauce flavors. Serve topped with the Cotija cheese.

Y LISTO AND ENJOY!

# MEXICAN WEDDING MACARONI SALAD

**Prep time: 15 minutes**
**Cook time: 10 minutes**
**SERVES 8 TO 10**

1 (16-ounce) package elbow macaroni pasta

2 medium carrots, shredded

1 (15.5-ounce) can corn, drained

3 tablespoons mayonnaise

2 tablespoons freshly ground black pepper

1 tablespoon Tapatio hot sauce

Fresh cilantro sprigs, for garnish

If it's an old-school, traditional Mexican wedding where the parents are involved, you will find this pasta on the menu 95 percent of the time. This simple recipe pairs perfectly with the typical main dishes like birria or mole, or anything saucy and spicy.

It all goes back to the old days in Mexico, when a padrino, godfather or a sponsor, would help you feed the wedding guests by contributing a dish. They used very inexpensive ingredients, and they would make the best of what they could afford. Chicken was less expensive back then, so they'd often make a mole, or if you were lucky enough to have a cow you could make a birria. The addition of hot sauce is my Michoacan mother's family secret. The vinegar and spices are subtle but give it a little kick that elevates the other flavors. (So glad I caught them adding that!)

1 • Bring a large pot of water to a boil and boil the pasta per package directions. Drain.

2 • Transfer the pasta to a large, shallow serving bowl, and allow it to cool, about 7 minutes. Add the carrots, corn, mayonnaise, pepper, and our secret ingredient, the hot sauce; toss it all together. Garnish with sprigs of cilantro.

**Y LISTO AND ENJOY!**

# CHILE RELLENOS

BATTERED PEPPERS STUFFED WITH CHEESE

Prep time: 35 minutes
Cook time: 15 minutes

SERVES 6 TO 8

8 fresh poblano chiles

1 pound (16 ounces) queso fresco, sliced into long, ½-inch-thick strips to fit into the peppers

½ cup all-purpose flour

6 large eggs, room temperature

1 teaspoon salt

2 cups canola oil

Serve with your choice of rice, beans, and/or salsa

When meat was scarce, poblano peppers and eggs (at least back then!) were affordable. Eating meat may have been reserved for a celebratory event, but this traditional recipe gets deliciously creative, stuffing the peppers with cheese and coating them in an egg batter before frying. When poblano peppers go on sale we buy them all up and have chile rellenos once a week. And we don't eat meat on Fridays for forty days during lent, so this dish is on heavy rotation that time of year, too.

You can stuff them with ground beef, chicken, or even turkey if you prefer. And you can bake them without the egg batter, like you would stuffed bell peppers. Some like to add chile rellenos to a caldito, a soup or a stew made with blended tomatoes, garlic, onion, oregano or sage, and chicken stock. You essentially garnish the bowl with a whole battered and fried chile! Others like to make a really spicy tomato sauce and drizzle it on top, or a creamy avocado sauce, or a chipotle sauce. Chile rellenos is also good stuffed with ground beef and raisins. The variations are endless.

1 • Heat a large comal or skillet over medium-high heat, and cook the poblanos, turning occasionally, until they are charred on all sides, about 6 minutes. (Alternatively, you can char them on the stovetop directly over a low open flame.) Remove from the heat. Put the poblanos in gallon-size, resealable plastic bags, and allow to sweat for 10 minutes to help loosen the skin. Peel away the charred layer of skin. Slice lengthwise on one side, keeping the stems intact, to open a pocket and remove the seeds.

2 • Heat a large comal or skillet over medium-high heat, and cook the poblanos, turning occasionally, until they are charred on all sides, about 6 minutes. (Alternatively, you can char them on the stovetop directly over a low open flame.) Remove from the heat. Put the poblanos in gallon-size, resealable plastic bags, and allow to sweat for 10 minutes to help loosen the skin. Peel away the charred layer of skin. Slice lengthwise on one side, keeping the stems intact, to open a pocket and remove the seeds.

3 • Stuff each of the poblanos with 3 to 4 queso strips. Close the stuffed pods securely with toothpicks, threading one toothpick through per pod. Lightly dust all sides of the stuffed peppers with flour and set aside.

4 • Separate the yolks and the egg whites between two medium bowls. Whisk the egg whites with an electric stand mixer or hand mixer on high until peaks form. Another way of testing if the egg whites are ready is to (carefully) flip the bowl upside down. The egg whites should not fall or slide off. Add the yolks and salt to the whipped whites and whisk again on low speed until combined.

5 • Heat the oil in a large skillet over medium-high heat. Check the heat by dipping a wooden spoon into the hot oil; if it sizzles, it's ready. Dip the filled and flour-dusted chiles, one at a time, into the egg mixture until well coated. Immediately, but carefully, place the coated poblanos in the hot oil; fry until golden brown, turning once, or until the batter is completely cooked on both sides, about 2 minutes per side. Set aside to drain on paper towels, to absorb the excess oil. Repeat until all of the poblanos are fried. Remove the toothpicks.

6 • Arrange the chile rellenos on a large platter. Serve with your preferred rice, beans, and/or salsa.

Y LISTO AND ENJOY!

# MEXICAN BUFFALO CHICKEN BURRITO

Prep time: 20 minutes
Cook time: 15 minutes

SERVES 6

½ cup canola oil

4 boneless, skinless chicken breasts, cut into ½-inch cubes

2 tablespoons ground paprika

2 tablespoons dried oregano

2 tablespoons garlic salt

1 cup shredded Mexican blend cheese

4 ounces cream cheese, room temperature

2 tablespoons Frank's Red Hot hot sauce

2 tablespoons ranch dressing

6 (10-inch) flour tortillas

4 cups Refried Beans (page 157)

4 cups Mexican Red Rice (page 146)

3 cups shredded iceberg lettuce

1 white onion, diced

1 bunch fresh cilantro leaves, roughly chopped

1 cup sour cream

I've always packed my husband's lunch during the work week. It's the easiest thing for him, as he only has thirty minutes to eat. I think he's a bit spoiled, because on days when I run out of time or food and suggest he just grab a hamburger, he complains that it's not the same and prefers to just go without, saying, "I will just wait until I come home." So, I get creative, and burritos are perfect for quick and easy lunches. Instead of the typical carne asada, I take inspiration where I can find it; this recipe came from seeing someone serve buffalo chicken and I thought, I can make this my own in a burrito. Give packed burrito lunches a try, the essentials will always be rice and beans, and you'll find leftover meats can work really well with some pico de gallo.

1 • Heat the oil in a large pan over medium-high heat. Check the heat by dipping your wooden spoon into the hot oil; if it sizzles, it's ready. Add the chicken and cook, stirring frequently, until lightly golden brown, about 4 minutes. Stir in the paprika, oregano, and garlic salt; continue cooking, stirring frequently, until fully browned on all sides, about 5 more minutes.

2 • In a large bowl, combine the cooked chicken, Mexican cheese, cream cheese, hot sauce, and ranch dressing. Mix well.

3 • Heat a large, dry comal or skillet over medium-high heat. Place a tortilla on the comal and heat it until it bubbles on top then flip it over, about 30 seconds on each side. Place the warm tortilla on a flat surface and build the burrito. Layer the beans, then the rice, and the creamy chicken mixture horizontally across the center. Top with some of the lettuce, onion, cilantro, and a drizzle of sour cream. To wrap your burrito, fold the sides in toward to middle, then wrap the top and bottom around the filling, nice and tight. Slice in half. Repeat with the remaining tortillas.

Y LISTO AND ENJOY!

MEXICAN BEEF CHILI

# CHiLE CON CARNE

Prep time: 15 minutes
Cook time: 45 minutes

SERVES 8 TO 10

I got married at a very young age. I was seventeen and my husband was nineteen. My dad told him, just wait two more months and she'll be eighteen! But we couldn't wait, and my dad signed for me. Chili con carne was the first recipe I learned from my mother-in-law, so my husband could be reminded of his mom's cooking. She has a very different style from my mother. My mom, Bertha, is Michoacan which is known for indigenous herbs and spices combined with meats. While my mother-in-law, Victoria, is from Compostela Nayarit, where they use citrusy and spicy foods and lots of garlic and onions. They're both good cooks but use different techniques. You'll find this chili is super spicy. Adjust the heat to your liking by using less chiles de árbol.

1 tablespoon canola oil

3 pounds sirloin beef, cut into short, 1-inch strips

2 teaspoons salt

1 white onion, thinly sliced, plus ¼ whole white onion

3 Roma tomatoes

2 garlic cloves

10 chiles de árbol, or as many as desired

1 tablespoon chicken bouillon powder

¼ bunch fresh cilantro

Serve with Mexican Red Rice (page 146) or beans as a side dish

1 • Heat the oil in a large pan over medium-high heat, and cook the beef, stirring frequently, until browned, about 10 minutes. Season the meat with the salt, then add the sliced onion; mix well and cook, stirring, until the onion is translucent, about 4 minutes.

2 • While the meat is cooking, char the tomatoes and garlic on a medium, dry comal or skillet over medium-high heat, about 3 minutes on each side. Set aside. On the same dry, hot comal, toast the chiles de árbol until they just begin to darken but before they begin to smoke, moving and flipping until toasted on all sides, about 3 minutes. (Remove immediately as they can burn easily, and you don't want your family coughing from that chile-spiked smoke!)

3 • Transfer the tomatoes, garlic, and chiles de árbol to a blender. Add the remaining onion, the chicken bouillon powder, and 1 cup of water and blend until smooth. Set aside.

4 • Once you see all the liquid from the beef has been absorbed, it is ready. Add the chile sauce and the cilantro to the meat and mix well; bring the mixture to a simmer to allow the flavors to meld, about 10 minutes.

5 • Serve with red rice or beans.

Y LISTO AND ENJOY!

# MEXICAN CORN IN A CUP

# ESQUITE

Prep time: 10 minutes
Cook time: 55 minutes
SERVES 6 TO 8

8 fresh white corn ears

1 tablespoon salt

1 tablespoon granulated sugar

1 stick (8 tablespoons) unsalted butter

Tapatio hot sauce (optional)

1 cup shredded Cotija cheese

1 cup mayonnaise

8 teaspoons chile powder

Juice of 2 limes

## Equipment
8 wooden skewers

8 mason jars or tall glasses

The elote man can be found on the streets of Mexico and in LA. They walk around with a cart and sell corn on the cob or corn like this, in a cup. Nowadays, you can also find places that are a bit like ice cream shops but instead sell all these street foods, including chamango (spicy mango in a cup like a slushy). The elote man is evolving. But every kid knows the sound of the bell if he passes by, and people run out like it's the ice cream truck. We still get them, and my kids get excited—but before they were $1 each and now it's literally $5 for one corn on the cob!

After they remove the kernels from the cob, they lightly char the corn in a hot pan, which lends a smoky flavor. My dad would always tell us to add a little sugar to the corn water to help sweeten it as it boils, as some are naturally sweet and some are not. These days people get creative and add crushed hot Cheetos or Takis to the top in place of the chile powder.

1 • Bring a large pot of water to a boil. While the water is coming to a boil, shuck the corn; discard the corn silk but reserve the fresh corn husks.

2 • Add the corn cobs, salt, and sugar to the boiling water; add more water to cover, if necessary. Fully cover the corn with the fresh husks—this adds flavor to the cooking water and creates a steam blanket. Cover the pot with a lid and cook until the ears are completely tender and a broth has formed, about 45 minutes. Remove the corn from the pot and set aside to cool for 5 minutes. Reserve 1 cup of the corn broth.

3 • Take a wooden skewer and insert it into the middle of what was the stem end of the cooked corn. Use the skewer as a handle to help you hold the corn in place and then cut the kernels off the cobs with a knife.

4 • Heat a dry cast-iron skillet or comal over medium-high heat, and cook half of the kernels, stirring constantly, until they are lightly charred, 3 to 5 minutes. Set aside and repeat with the second half.

5 • In another large pot, melt the butter over medium heat; stir in the corn and the reserved cup of broth.

6 • You can now begin to assemble your esquite in mason jars or tall glasses. I like to start by adding a couple dashes of hot sauce to each glass, then layering 1 tablespoon of cheese, ¼ cup of corn, and 1 tablespoon of mayonnaise. Repeat the layers until it's filled, and top off with 1 teaspoon chile powder, lime, and hot sauce.

# APPETIZERS

**Spicy Habanero Guacamole**

✦

**Mexican Queso**
(CHEESE DIP)

✦

**Mexican Bolillos**

✦

**Papas Rellenas**
(STUFFED BAKED POTATOES)

✦

**Guasanas**
(FRESH GREEN GARBANZOS)

✦

**Papitas Enchiladas**
(SMALL WAX POTATOES
IN CHILE SAUCE)

✦

**Pulpo
a las Brazas**
(GRILLED OCTOPUS
WITH CITRUS
GARLIC BUTTER)

✦

# SPiCY HABANERO GUACAMOLE

**Prep time: 15 minutes**
**Cook time: 2 minutes**
**SERVES 6 TO 8**

1 or 2 fresh habanero peppers

2 garlic cloves

2 teaspoons chicken bouillon powder

1 teaspoon flaky salt

4 large avocados

½ white onion, diced

2 Roma tomatoes, diced

½ bunch cilantro, chopped

Juice of 1 fresh lime

1 (14.5-ounce) bag tortilla chips

Avocado is one of the most used vegetables (technically, fruit!) in a Mexican household. It's like our butter. One day, I ran out of serrano chiles, which I typically used to make our guacamole, so I substituted a roasted habanero. My daughter said it was the best I had ever made, so I stuck with this recipe. Habanero is super hot but also sweet. I use one or two—one is safer from a spice standpoint—and roasted garlic, too. My family can't get enough. I always use a molcajete to make this, but if you have to you could use a blender.

1 • Roast the habaneros and garlic over an open flame until soft and charred, about 2 minutes. In a large molcajete, start by grinding the garlic, chicken bouillon powder, and salt. Add the habaneros and grind the mixture until you attain a creamy consistency. Add the scooped-out avocado flesh. Reserve the avocado pits. Use a spoon to mix in the avocado, then mash until the mixture is mostly creamy but some chunks of avocado remain.

2 • Add the onion, tomatoes, and cilantro, lightly mashing the mixture but not until it becomes creamy, just a little bit to release the flavors, leaving it a bit chunky. Squeeze in the lime juice and mix well with a spoon. Add the avocado pits. As my mother says, the pits will help the guacamole stay fresh and green. Enjoy with tortilla chips.

**Y LISTO AND ENJOY**

# MEXICAN QUESO

**Prep time: 10 minutes**
**Cook time: 20 minutes**

**SERVES 6 TO 8**

I have two men and two boys in my house, and they are always watching sports. Cheese dips are the fastest things for me to throw into the oven around game time or during a family gathering. I use whatever cheese I have on hand. It's quick, and who doesn't like cheese with a kick of spices? It goes well with beer and chicken wings and keeps them entertained while I start the rest of the food.

½ pound Pepper Jack cheese, cut into ½-inch cubes

½ pound American cheese, cut into ½-inch cubes

½ pound Oaxaca cheese, separated into strings

1 (12-ounce) can evaporated milk

1 pickled jalapeño chile, minced

1 teaspoon chicken bouillon powder

½ cup canola oil

1 fresh jalapeño chile, sliced into rounds

1 (14.5-ounce) bag tortilla chips

1 • Preheat oven to 350°F.

2 • In a deep, medium cast-iron skillet, place the Pepper Jack, American, and Oaxaca cheeses, the evaporated milk, pickled jalapeño, and chicken bouillon powder; mix well. Transfer the skillet to the oven and bake until melted, about 15 minutes.

3 • While the queso is in the oven, heat the oil in a small frying pan over medium heat; when the oil is hot, add the fresh jalapeño rounds and fry until crispy, 3 to 5 minutes. Set aside to drain on paper towels. Remove the queso from the oven once it's nicely melted.

4 • Top it off with the fried jalapeño rounds and serve immediately with tortilla chips to enjoy the warm, melted cheese.

**Y LISTO AND ENJOY!**

# MEXICAN BOLILLOS

1 tablespoon granulated sugar

2¼ teaspoons (2 packets) instant yeast

1¼ cups warm water (120°F)

1 tablespoon canola oil, plus more for oiling

1 teaspoon salt

3½ cups bread flour, plus more for dusting

Prep time: 1 hour 50 minutes
Cook time: 30 minutes
MAKES 6 ROLLS

I was born in Chapala, Mexico, and the bolillos from there are still the best I have found. Twenty-five years later I brought my kids there for a visit and they fell in love with them, too, so I decided I had to try to re-create them at home. It wasn't easy to accomplish, figuring out the dough and the rising times, but I made it happen. These are Mexican sandwich breads that you can stuff with anything. It was poor man's food in my mother's time, as the bread really fills you up. If there was not enough meat in the house, people stuffed them with cheese or beans and made it a meal. And when they didn't have beans, they'd stuff them with jalapeños from a can. (I'm not a fan of those and imagine how spicy that is!) Growing up, my mother would make us torta de jamon, which is a classic sandwich made from ham ends, queso fresco, lettuce, and tomato. We would head to the park or public pools, and picnic on tortas. They're inexpensive, simple, and just so good—particularly when you're hungry from being in the water all morning. The bread is crispy and crunchy on the outside and really soft in the middle.

1 • Put the yeast into a medium bowl, stir in the warm water and sugar, then add the oil and salt and stir well. Immediately, using a rubber spatula, stir the flour into the wet ingredients until all of the liquid has been absorbed.

2 • On a lightly floured surface, knead the dough by stretching and pulling for 5 minutes. As the dough becomes smoother, begin to pull and flip the dough (lift the ball up with your fingers and allow the weight of the dough to stretch down as you lift it, then slap the dough back onto the table and repeat). Knead in this manner until the dough is elastic, about 5 minutes, then form the dough into a smooth ball. Put a generous amount of oil on your hands, then spread the oil all over the dough ball. Place it back in the bowl, then cover the bowl with plastic wrap. Allow the dough to rest until it has doubled in size, 45 to 60 minutes.

3 • Punch the air out of the dough with your fist, then transfer it to a flat, floured surface. Cut the dough into 6 triangular wedges. Pull the pointy ends of each wedge toward the middle to form 3-inch-diameter balls. Place the balls on a sheet tray lined with parchment paper and cover with plastic wrap. Set aside to rest for 10 minutes.

4 • Stretch each ball out flat until it is 8 to 10 inches long and about 3 inches wide, gently patting the dough down with your fingers. Place one of the dough pieces vertically on the table in front of you. From the bottom

(recipe continues)

end, fold the dough up 1 inch, then take either side of that fold, the bottom corners, and pull those corners up and toward one another, so you form a point on the bottom edge of the dough. Then fold that point or triangle up. Flatten the dough gently with your fingers, then repeat the process of taking the bottom corners and folding the dough into a point. This is repeated until you have 1 inch of flat dough left at the top. Stretch and fold that piece down, wrapping over the dough until it fully covers the log. Pinch the loose ends closed on the sides and corners and gently roll the dough until you form it into the bolillo shape, about 8 inches long. Dust the dough with flour and transfer to a baking sheet. Cover with plastic wrap and let the dough rest for 30 minutes.

5 • Preheat the oven to 375°F.

6 • Using a sharp knife, slice a shallow slit lengthwise down the top of each bolillo. Brush each slit with oil. Bake for about 30 minutes, or until lightly golden brown. Allow to cool for 3 minutes. Enjoy them while still nice and warm. Beautiful!

Y LISTO AND ENJOY!

# STUFFED BAKED POTATOES

# PAPAS RELLENAS

Prep time: 15 minutes
Cook time: 1 hour 30 minutes
SERVES 6 TO 8

8 Russet potatoes

4 tablespoons olive oil

1 teaspoon salt

2 pounds (80/20) ground beef

1 white onion, diced

1 garlic clove, minced

1 tablespoon freshly ground black pepper

1 tablespoon Mesa Mia: Jenny's Favorite Seasoning

2 cups shredded cheddar cheese

## Toppings

Fresh chopped cilantro

Diced white onion

Sour cream

Chile de Aceite (page 174)

When we get tired of tacos, I pull out this recipe. It brings back a lot of memories, as it was one of the first things I started to make after getting married. My husband was making $6 an hour and we couldn't afford a steak, so my go-to ingredients were ground beef and tomatoes. I'd try to impress him with my creativity within our budget. Now that I have more money, sometimes I stuff it with carne asada. Also, these work great as appetizers.

## COOK'S NOTE

Don't throw away the scooped-out, cooked potato. You can use it to make potato taquitos. Just mix it with cream cheese or Monterey or Oaxacan cheese, butter, and a little chicken bouillon powder. Stuff some tortillas, then roll them up and fry.

1 • Preheat the oven to 350°F.

2 • Wash the potatoes, then pat dry. With a fork, poke holes all over the potatoes to allow the entire potato to cook from the inside out. Drizzle with olive oil and season with the salt and pepper. For the potatoes to bake evenly, place them directly on a rack with a baking sheet placed on the rack underneath. Bake for about 1 hour, or until fully cooked.

3 • Meanwhile, in a large skillet over medium heat, cook the ground beef, breaking it up with spoon, until browned, about 10 minutes. Drain any excess oil from the pan. Add the onion, garlic, pepper, and seasoning. Mix well and cook, stirring frequently, until the onion is soft and the flavors have melded, about 10 minutes.

4 • Once the potatoes are cooked, carefully cut a rectangular section out of the top of each of the potatoes lengthwise, to create a "canoe." Scoop out some of the flesh to make room for the meat (see Cook's Note). Stuff the potatoes with the meat and top off with the cheese. Place on a large baking sheet and bake for 10 minutes, or until the cheese has fully melted. Garnish with cilantro, onion, sour cream, and Chile de Aceite, as desired.

Y LISTO AND ENJOY!

## FRESH GREEN GARBANZOS

# GUASANAS

Prep time: 5 minutes
Cook time: 20 minutes
SERVES 8 TO 10

3 pounds fresh green garbanzos

1 tablespoon flaky salt, plus more for topping

Tapatio hot sauce, for serving

1 to 2 fresh limes, cut in wedges

In Jalisco, where my parents are from, these are known as guasanas instead of garbanzos because they're fresh and still in the pod. They are sold on the streets of Mexico, dry roasted and salted. They get a bit charred on the outside of the pod and are served in a paper cone made from newspaper, with hot sauce and lime juice. People will chew on them, pod and all, to get the most flavor (but you don't swallow the pod, you spit that part out).

1 • Heat a large disco (or a large, shallow frying pan, comal, wok, or Dutch oven) over medium heat. Place the garbanzos, still in their pods (do not add water) into the disco. Add the salt and, using two wooden spoons, stir continuously until the pods are charred, about 10 minutes. Then cover with a large pot lid and steam, stirring every 2 to 3 minutes to prevent burning, until they are cooked through, about 10 minutes. Beautiful.

2 • Serve in a paper cone or use a paper cup. Top with more flaky salt, hot sauce, and a squeeze lime juice all over.

Y LISTO AND ENJOY!

# SMALL WAX POTATOES IN CHILE SAUCE

# PAPITAS ENCHILADAS

Prep time: 10 minutes
Cook time: 30 minutes

SERVES 8 TO 10

2 pounds baby wax potatoes (grape size)

1 tablespoon salt

12 dried chiles de árbol

2 dried morita chiles

1 cup fresh lime juice

2 garlic cloves

1 tablespoon Mesa Mia: Jenny's Favorite Seasoning

1 tablespoon chicken bouillon powder

2 tablespoons unsalted butter

## Equipment

Box of toothpicks

In restaurants in Mexico, they serve these little round wax potatoes instead of chips. They're great appetizers with a beer on a hot day, and so addicting! I use really tiny potatoes for this recipe, like grape size. They're boiled to a perfect, not too mushy, soft texture, and you can eat the skin and all. You can make these with a green salsa, too, they're both good but the chile de árbol is super spicy, like fire, and you gotta wash it down with a big gulp of beer.

1 • Bring a large pot of water to a boil; add the potatoes and salt and cook until the potatoes are cooked through, about 15 minutes. Drain and set aside.

2 • Meanwhile, to a blender, add the chile de árbol, moritas, lime juice, garlic, seasoning, and chicken bouillon powder and blend until smooth. Set aside.

3 • In a medium pan, melt the butter over medium-low heat. Add the cooked potatoes and give them a quick stir, then stir in the chile de árbol mixture. Cover the pan and simmer the mixture to allow the potatoes to absorb all the flavors and spices, about 7 minutes. Transfer the mixture to a serving bowl and enjoy eating these using toothpicks to spear them. This is a perfect appetizer with a cold beer and a great crowd-pleaser!

Y LISTO AND ENJOY!

# GRILLED OCTOPUS WITH CITRUS GARLIC BUTTER

# PULPO A LAS BRAZAS

Prep time: 15 minutes

Cook time: 1 hour

SERVES 4 TO 6

My dad, brother, and now my son, all make this dish. It's an appetizer we have, alongside tostadas, when family is together. Or it could be dinner if you have a lot. Regardless, when we have seafood going on we have to have grilled octopus. In our house, the guys make it while the women finish the rest of the food. Enjoy this with a nice, cold beer.

4 pounds whole octopus, head on

½ white onion

6 garlic cloves plus 1 garlic head, minced, divided

3 dried bay leaves

2 teaspoons salt

1 stick (8 tablespoons) unsalted butter, melted

Juice of ½ orange

Juice of 1 fresh lime

## Toppings

Tapatio hot sauce (optional)

Lime wedges, for serving

1 • Start by cleaning the octopus. Remove the eyes and beak. Fill a medium pot with water over medium-high heat. Add the onion, 6 garlic cloves, bay leaves, and salt and bring to a boil. Add the octopus by holding the octopus head and dipping the tentacles only the boiling water for 3 seconds; pull them out and repeat this 3 more times. Then add the entire octopus to the water and boil for 45 minutes. Drain and set aside.

2 • Heat a grill to medium.

3 • In a small saucepan over medium-low heat, combine the butter, the minced garlic, orange juice, and lime juice. Mix well.

4 • Char the octopus on the grill until grill marks appear and the thickest tentacles are tender, 2 to 3 minutes per side. Brush the octopus continuously with the citrus garlic butter while cooking. It will turn a nice, deep purple color.

5 • Slice the octopus, starting with the tentacles, into ½- to 1-inch pieces. Serve with the remaining garlic butter as a dipping sauce. I like to eat it with a drizzle of Tapatio hot sauce and extra lime juice.

Y LISTO AND ENJOY!

# TACOS, TAQUITOS & TAMALES

**♦♦♦♦♦♦♦♦♦♦♦♦♦♦♦♦♦♦♦♦♦♦♦♦♦♦♦♦♦♦♦♦♦♦♦♦♦♦♦♦♦**

## Quesabirria Tacos

♦

## Tacos de Camaron, Baja Style
(BATTERED SHRIMP TACOS)

♦

## Tacos de Canasta– Carne Deshebrada, Papa con Chorizo, y Frijoles
(3 BASKET-STYLE TACOS)

♦

## Tacos de Alambre
(MEATY STRINGY CHEESE TACOS)

♦

## Tacos de Lengua
(BEEF TONGUE TACOS)

♦

## Tacos de Tripas
(BEEF INTESTINE TACOS)

♦

## Taquitos de Papa
(FRIED POTATO TAQUITOS)

♦

## Taquitos de Carne con Chipotle y Queso Oaxaca
(BEEF TAQUITOS WITH CHIPOTLE AND CHEESE)

♦

## Tamales de Puerco en Chile Rojo
(RED CHILI PORK TAMALES)

♦

## Tamales de Pollo Salsa Verde
(GREEN SALSA CHICKEN TAMALES)

♦

## Tamales de 3 Rajas
(3-PEPPER CHEESE TAMALES)

♦

## Tamales de Elote
(SWEET CORN TAMALES)

# QUESABIRRIA TACOS

Prep time: 5 minutes
Cook time: about 25 minutes
SERVES 8

8 cups birria broth plus 2 pounds Birria de Res (Mexican Beef Stew) meat (see page 130)

½ cup canola oil, divided

16 (6-inch) corn tortillas

4 cups shredded Oaxaca cheese

1 bunch fresh cilantro, roughly chopped

1 white onion, diced

Tapatio hot sauce, for serving

4 fresh limes, cut into wedges

This recipe is part of what put me on the map. The first viral video was my mom's birria, and from there I made these because leftover birria meat always makes a great taco. The inspiration to create this mashup came from having been asked in Mexico if I wanted a carne asada taco, like a quesadilla with a taco. And the broth dipping idea originated from having seen one of my uncles make tacos stuffed with other meat, as the birria meat always went fast, and then he'd drizzle the leftover birria broth on top. Now, I make sure to have leftover birria meat just to make quesabirria tacos.

I use corn tortillas instead of the typical flour used to make quesadillas because the corn gets so crispy and crunchy, and tastes so good dipped in the broth. In the end, this recipe went even more viral than the birria!

1 • Start by skimming the red fat from the surface of the birria broth (this fat comes from the meat). Transfer the fat to a large, shallow bowl and set aside. Transfer the birria meat to a cutting board. Reserve the broth. Chop the meat and set aside.

2 • Heat the oil in a large comal or skillet over medium heat. Using tongs, dip a tortilla into the reserved red fat until it is lightly coated in a red layer of fat. BEAUTIFUUUULLL!!!! Hold the tortilla up to allow some of the fat to drip off and then quickly place it on the hot comal. Immediately start building the taco by adding ¼ cup of the cheese and about 3 tablespoons of the chopped meat on top of tortilla; fold it over. Fry the taco until nice and crispy and cheese has melted, about 3 minutes on each side. Set the tacos aside on paper towels to absorb any excess oil. Repeat with the remaining tortillas, cheese, and meat.

3 • Stuff the tacos with cilantro and onion, and add hot sauce and lime juice. Serve the broth in a small dipping bowl, also garnished with cilantro, onion, hot sauce, and a squeeze of fresh lime juice. Now dip the quesabirria taco in the warm birria broth.

Y LISTO AND ENJOY!

# TACOS DE CAMARON, BAJA STYLE

Prep time: 1 hour 15 minutes
Cook time: 30 minutes
SERVES 10

Here's another taco that we need to have every time we go to Ensenada. We have a favorite spot we go to, but we like my cousin Erika's way better. I'm so happy she shared it with me.

2 pounds jumbo shrimp, peeled and deveined

2 tablespoons Mesa Mia: Jenny's Favorite Seasoning

2 cups all-purpose flour

1 (12.5-ounce) bottle mineral water

1 (12-ounce) bottle beer, (I like Modelo but any beer is OK)

2 tablespoons chicken bouillon powder

2 tablespoons garlic powder

2 tablespoons freshly ground black pepper

2 tablespoons yellow mustard

4 cups shredded green cabbage

2 Roma tomatoes, diced

1 white onion, chopped

1 bunch of cilantro, chopped

Juice of 2 fresh limes

4 cups canola oil

20 (6-inch) corn tortillas, warmed

## Toppings

Mayonnaise

Aguacate Chile (page 70)

Sour cream

Lime wedges

1 • Butterfly the shrimp, slicing down the back but not all the way through and leaving the tail section intact. Pat the shrimp dry and place it into a medium bowl. Sprinkle with the seasoning and set aside.

2 • To prepare the batter, in a large bowl, combine the flour, mineral water, beer, chicken bouillon powder, garlic powder, black pepper, and mustard; mix until the flour lumps have dissolved. The batter should be smooth and not too thick. Toss the shrimp into the bowl with the batter and set aside while you prep the cabbage salad.

3 • In a separate medium bowl, add the cabbage, tomatoes, onions, cilantro, and lime, and toss until well combined. Set aside.

4 • In a large, deep frying pan, heat the oil over medium heat. Check your heat by dipping a wooden spoon into the hot oil; if it sizzles, it's ready. Fry the battered shrimp in batches of six, so as not to overcrowd the pan, until golden brown, about 3 minutes on each side.

Drain on paper towels. Repeat with the remaining shrimp.

5 • To assemble the tacos, I like to start by spreading mayonnaise on a warmed tortilla, then I add the fried shrimp and top it with the cabbage salad, Aguacate Chile, sour cream, and a squeeze of lime juice.

Y LISTO AND ENJOY!

# TACOS DE CANASTA

## CARNE DESHEBRADA,
## PAPA CON CHORIZO, Y FRIJOLES

**Prep time: 3 hours**
**Cook time: 3 hours**
**SERVES 10 TO 12**

These tacos were conceived by Mexican street vendors who weren't able to afford a taco stand. Instead, they layer the tacos in a basket, one flavor for each layer, pour the hot oil over the top, cover them to hold in the steam and keep them soft—then tie the whole basket to their bicycles. As they ride through town they call out, "tacos de canasta!" It's a bit like Uber Eats, you run out at lunch time and buy three or four when you hear them come calling.

### NOTE

Deshebrada translates to shredded beef.

2 pounds flank roast (thick cut is best, too thin will dry out)

½ white onion

1 garlic head

4 dried bay leaves

1 tablespoon plus 1 teaspoon salt, divided

4 Russet potatoes

1 (8-ounce) pork chorizo chub

2 cups canola oil, divided

24 (6-inch) corn tortillas

2 cups Refried Beans (page 157)

### Red Chile Sauce

1 Roma tomato

4 guajillo chiles, seeds removed

¼ white onion

2 garlic cloves

1 teaspoon black peppercorns

1 tablespoon chicken bouillon powder

### Toppings

Red Salsa (page 9)

Thinly sliced fried onions

### Equipment

4 large sheets parchment paper or foil

2 kitchen towels

1 • In a large, tall pot, bring 8 cups of water, the beef, ½ onion, garlic, bay leaves, and 1 tablespoon of salt to a boil over medium-high heat. Cover and cook until soft and tender, for 2½ to 3 hours.

2 • While the meat is cooking, make the Red Chile Sauce: in a small saucepan bring the tomato, guajillos, and water to cover to a boil over medium-high heat. Cook until softened, about 8 minutes. Drain and transfer the guajillos and tomato to a blender with 3 cups of the beef broth from the pot, the black peppercorns, and the chicken bouillon powder. Blend until smooth. Set aside.

3 • In a medium saucepan over medium-high heat, bring the potatoes and enough water to cover to a boil. Boil until soft and mashable, about 20 minutes. Drain the potatoes, then peel and discard the skins. In a large bowl, mash the potatoes with the 1 teaspoon of salt.

4 • In a small skillet, cook the chorizo over medium-high heat, stirring constantly, until browned, about 8 minutes. Mix the chorizo with the mashed potatoes and set aside.

5 • Once the beef is cooked, remove the meat from the pot, and allow to cool down for a few minutes. Shred the beef. Put the beef in a bowl, add 2 cups of the red chile sauce and mix well; set aside.

6 • Prepare a large Dutch oven pot by lining the bottom and sides with a kitchen towel, the corners flopping out over the top. Next, layer 2 to 3 large pieces of parchment paper or foil sheets on top of kitchen towel, going up the sides and overlapping the sheets to be nice and tight. Set aside.

7 • In a medium pan, heat 1 cup of oil over medium-high heat. Check your heat by dipping your wooden spoon into the hot oil; if it sizzles, you're ready. Lightly fry the tortillas one at a time for 10 seconds to soften; stack on a plate as you go.

8 • Fill 8 tortillas with red chili beef and fold in half. Then fill 8 tortillas with the chorizo potatoes and the remaining 8 with the refried beans. Arrange the folded tacos in a circular pattern in the prepared Dutch oven. Arrange it so that each layer is a different flavor. (When I am doing a double batch, I stack them in circular layers all the way to the top of the oven if needed.)

9 • Heat the remaining 1 cup of oil over medium-high heat until boiling hot. Drizzle the hot oil directly over the top of the stacked tacos in the Dutch oven. Immediately, cover tightly with the parchment or foil and the second kitchen towel. Cover with the Dutch oven lid and allow it to steam like this for 10 minutes. Serve with red salsa and top with fried onions

Y LISTO AND ENJOY!

# TACOS DE ALAMBRE

Prep time: 25 minutes
Cook time: 40 minutes

**SERVES 6 TO 8**

½ pound bacon, cut in 1-inch pieces

1 pound skirt steak, cut in 1-inch pieces

1 tablespoon Mesa Mia: Jenny's Favorite Seasoning

1½ pounds pork chorizo

1 white onion, diced

1 red bell pepper, diced

1 fresh serrano chile, diced

½ cup shredded Oaxaca cheese

½ cup shredded Menonita cheese

24 (3-inch) corn tortillas

Tapatio hot sauce or a favorite salsa (optional)

This is like a dip, because the way you eat this is straight out of the skillet. You don't even need a plate. Grab a tortilla and scoop it out. Top it with hot sauce and you're done. "Alambre" translates to cables or wires, because when you scoop out the meat and cheese, you'll see that the cheese stretches so much it looks just like that!

1 • In a medium cast-iron skillet over medium heat, fry the bacon, stirring constantly, until crispy, 10 to 12 minutes. Set the bacon aside to drain on paper towels. Reserve 1 teaspoon of bacon fat in the skillet, and drain the rest. Season the steak with the seasoning, then add it to the skillet over medium heat, stirring constantly, until just cooked through, about 10 minutes. Add the chorizo and cook, stirring frequently, until fully browned, 12 to 15 minutes.

2 • Stir in the bacon and add the onion, bell pepper, and serrano and cook, stirring, until vegetables are crisp-tender, about 3 minutes. Add the Oaxaca and Menonita cheeses, distributing the two types evenly on top; once the cheese melts, it's ready. Warm the tortillas on a dry comal or skillet over medium heat until beginning to crisp but still pliable and foldable.

3 • The way you eat this: place the skillet in the center of the table and have the warm tortillas in a tortillero next to the skillet. Grab a tortilla and use it to scoop up the meat. Enjoy it like an appetizer. You can top it with hot sauce or salsa, if desired. No plates needed

**Y LISTO AND ENJOY!**

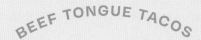

# TACOS DE LENGUA

Prep time: 45 hour
Cook time: 2 hours 30 minutes
SERVES 6 TO 8

People hover around the taco stands in Mexico, and the variety is wide; some specialize in just tongue, for example. There are so many ways to prepare beef tacos, coming from every part of the cow, but this is one of the three most popular. The tongue is a tough, lean cut, and has a layer you have to peel off after it's cooked. (And yes, they're ugly looking.) Instead of chopping the meat you can cube it, but I like to cook it longer to make it very tender, then finely chop it up.

## COOK'S NOTE

You will have plenty of time to prepare both salsas as the meat cooks.

1 (3 to 4 pounds) beef tongue

4 dried puya chiles

2 Roma tomatoes, halved

1 white onion, halved

1 head garlic

6 dried chiltepin chiles

2 fresh gueros chile (yellow banana peppers)

2 dried bay leaves

2 tablespoons salt

1 tablespoon whole black peppercorns

1 tablespoon dried oregano

24 (3-inch) corn tortillas, warmed

### Toppings

½ cabbage head, shredded

1 red onion, diced

1 bunch fresh cilantro, roughly chopped

5 fresh limes, cut into wedges

4 fresh guero chiles, diced

Dad's Tomatillo Salsa (page 179)

Salsa Taquera (page 170)

1 • Put the whole tongue in an 8-quart pot and add water until the meat is completely covered. Add the puyas, 2 tomatoes, white onion, garlic, chiltepins, gueros, bay leaves, salt, peppercorns, and oregano. Cover the pot tightly with a lid and cook until very tender, 2½ hours.

2 • Remove the meat and set it aside on a cutting board until cool enough to handle. Peel off the outer layer or skin of the tongue and discard. Shred the meat with your fingers or with a fork. Serve on a platter with individual bowls of the toppings surrounding the platter for presentation: cabbage, red onion, cilantro, limes, chile guero, salsa verde, and Salsa Taquera. Serve on the warm tortillas (place tortillas on a tortillero to keep warm) or stuff the tortillas, then heat the tacos in oil for 1 minute on each side.

Y LISTO AND ENJOY!

# BEEF INTESTINE TACOS

## TACOS DE TRIPAS

Prep time: 30 minutes
Cook time: 1 hour 45 minutes

SERVES 6 TO 8

12 pounds tripas de leche or small intestines from a mature cow

½ cup white vinegar

Juice of 2 fresh limes

1 medium white onion

1 head garlic

3 tablespoons salt

3 dried bay leaves

24 (6-inch) corn tortillas

Toppings

Cilantro leaves

½ medium white onion, minced

Ahumada Salsa Morita (page 178)

4 fresh limes, cut into wedges

Some of my cousins own taco stands and restaurants, and they have taught me that this is the very best way to make their customer favorite, tacos de tripas. In fact, they say you're not a real taco man if these aren't on your menu. It's another "poor man's food" that has become a delicacy—plus, it's packed with nutrition. Love them or hate them, they must be done properly. First, make sure you buy the less intense (from a smell and flavor stand-point) tripas that come from the small, NOT the large, intestines from a mature cow. Nevertheless, they will still smell a bit, so cleaning them first with vinegar and lime juice is essential or you will have some funky aromas flowing through your house. Tripas are sold braided to be more manageable. The secret is to never, ever unbraid them before boiling. This is a common mistake. If you cut them when you clean them, all the insides of the intestines spill out. The boiling sets the insides, then you can cut them into long strips for frying. Think of the insides almost like bone marrow. It's where the flavor lives. Otherwise all you're left with are rubbery intestines. Twelve pounds may seem like a lot, but it cooks way down and will seem more like six pounds by the end.

1 • Tripas (intestines) come in braids; do not separate the strands. To clean them, place the braids in a large pot and toss with the vinegar and lime juice. Set aside to marinate for 15 minutes. This helps to remove any bad odors. Drain and then give them a quick rinse.

2 • In a large disco (Mexican shallow fryer) or large skillet, bring the tripas, still in their braids, enough water to cover the tripas, the onion, garlic, salt, and bay leaves to a boil over medium-high heat. Cook the tripas until well done, 45 to 60 minutes.

3 • Once the tripas are done cooking, remove them from the disco or skillet and set aside. Reserve 1 cup of the tripas fat by using a large spoon and skimming it from the top of the tripas broth. Drain the remaining broth from the disco or skillet.

4 • Once they are cool enough to handle, cut the tripas into long strips. Reheat the reserved cup of fat in the disco or skillet over high heat; fry the strips of tripas to your desired level of crispiness, cooking in batches so as not to overcrowd. I like mine dark brown and extra crispy, so I fry them for about 25 minutes. As you go, set the hot tripas aside in an aluminum pan near the heat, to keep warm. Cut the tripas strips into 1-inch or bite-size pieces. Beautiful!!!!

(recipe continues on page 66)

5 • If you're using a disco, quickly dip one side of each tortilla in the leftover fat, then place the tortillas around the flat edge of the disco and allow them to heat until cooked but still soft and pliable, about 1 minute on each side. If you're not using a disco, heat a large, dry skillet over medium-high heat and heat the tortillas in the skillet after dipping them in the reserved fat. This will give your taco a whole different level of taste. Now let's eat! Serve the desired amount of tripas on a tortilla, top with cilantro, onion, Ahumada Salsa Morita, and squeeze lime juice all over!

Y LISTO AND ENJOY!

# FRIED POTATO TAQUITOS

# TAQUITOS DE PAPA

Prep time: 45 minutes
Cook time: 30 minutes
SERVES 6 TO 8

8 Russet potatoes

½ cup whole milk

4 ounces queso fresco, crumbled

2 tablespoons chicken bouillon powder

2 tablespoons sour cream

1 tablespoon unsalted butter

24 (6-inch) corn tortillas

2 cups canola oil, divided

## Toppings

Iceberg lettuce, shredded

Avocados, pitted, peeled, and sliced

Sour cream

Dad's Tomatillo Salsa (page 179) or Salsa Taquera (page 170)

Queso fresco, crumbled

These are one of the most popular tacos for lent, and they're vegetarian friendly for other times of the year. They're like a filler; they fill you up. You'll find them at most Mexican restaurants. I really like them, they're my go-to when I get tired of eating meat, alongside my bean tacos. So good, and they don't break the bank. Takes me back to my early days.

1 • Begin by rinsing, peeling, and and quartering the potatoes; they will cook faster. In a medium saucepan over medium-high heat, bring 4 cups of water to a boil and boil the potatoes until softened, about 12 minutes. To know whether the potatoes are fully cooked, insert a knife through the potato; if the knife goes in smoothly, they are ready.

2 • Drain the water, then to the same pot with the potatoes, add the milk, queso fresco, chicken bouillon powder, sour cream, and butter. Mash the mixture with a fork until all of the ingredients are combined. You should have a thick consistency.

3 • Before rolling the taquitos, make sure the tortillas are steamed and soft. The fastest way to steam tortillas is in resealable plastic bag in the microwave, 3 minutes for 24 tortillas. Immediately separate the tortillas so that they won't stick together. If you prefer not microwave then you can warm them on a dry comal or skillet (but it will take longer and not be as soft or roll as well!).

(recipe continues)

4 • Add 2 tablespoons, less is more for these, of potato mixture into the center of each tortilla and roll tightly. Don't over stuff as the potato mixture can ooze out.

5 • It's very important to shallow fry (oil should be halfway up the taquitos), otherwise the taquito will end up floating in the oil and come apart. In a large cast-iron pan, heat 1 cup of oil over medium heat. Check the heat by dipping a wooden spoon into the hot oil; if it sizzles, it's ready. Fry the taquitos in batches, adding more oil as needed, fold-side down, until crispy, about 3 minutes, then flip and fry until beautifully golden brown and crispy, another 2 minutes. Remove from the pan and place in a colander standing up to drain any excess oil.

6 • Serve the taquitos with lettuce, avocado, sour cream, salsa, and queso fresco.

Y LISTO AND ENJOY!

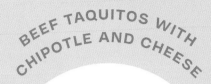

# TAQUITOS DE CARNE

## CON CHIPOTLE Y QUESO OAXACA

Prep time: 45 minutes
Cook time: 1 hour
**SERVES 6 TO 8**

We serve these with a very spicy chile and avocados mixture that goes beyond guacamole—it's just serranos and avocado! Sometimes I add ten instead of six serranos, but it can be like fire in your mouth. So, with six I am keeping it friendly. Adjust to your preferred heat level.

2 pounds (80/20) ground beef

1 (7-ounce) can chipotle peppers in adobo

2 garlic cloves, minced

2 tablespoons chicken bouillon powder

24 (6-inch) corn tortillas

1 pound Oaxaca cheese, cut into 2-inch pieces

2 cups canola oil, divided

### Aguacate Chile

½ cup water

2 avocados, pitted and peeled

6 fresh serrano chiles

1 tablespoon chicken bouillon powder

### Toppings

2 cups sour cream

1 • In a large cast-iron skillet over medium heat, cook the ground beef, stirring constantly and breaking it up with a spoon, until just browned, about 15 minutes. Drain off any excess oil from the skillet. Stir in the chipotle peppers in adobo, garlic, and chicken bouillon powder. As you mix, cut the chipotle peppers with the edge of the spoon.

2 • Make the Aguacate Chile: In a blender, add the water, avocados, serranos, and chicken bouillon powder. Blend until smooth.

3 • Before rolling the taquitos make sure the tortillas are steamed and soft. The fastest way to steam tortillas is in a resealable plastic bag in the microwave, 3 minutes for 24 tortillas. Immediately separate the tortillas so that they will not stick together. If you prefer not to use the microwave then you can warm them on a dry comal or skillet (but it will take longer and not be as soft or roll as well!).

4 • To each tortilla, add a piece of cheese in the middle along with 2 tablespoons of the chipotle meat mixture. Tightly roll each tortilla.

5 • In a large cast-iron pan, heat 1 cup of oil over medium heat. Check the heat by dipping a wooden spoon into the hot oil; if it sizzles, it's ready. Cooking in batches, adding more oil as needed with each batch, shallow fry the taquitos, beginning with the fold-side down to seal them, then flip them until all sides are golden brown and crispy, about 5 minutes. Remove the taquitos from the pan and place in a colander, standing up, to drain any excess oil.

6 • Present all the taquitos on a large, beautiful platter. Now we're ready to serve! To prepare your taquitos, drizzle the Aguacate Chile on top, along with the sour cream. They can also be dipped in the Aguacate Chile.

Y LISTO AND ENJOY!

# TAMALES DE PUERCO EN CHILE ROJO

Prep time: 1 hour 20 minutes
Cook time: 3 hours

**SERVES 10 TO 12**

My mother's side of the family brought us the tradition of tamale making every Christmas. On the twenty-third, we all come together and prep the tamales for Christmas Eve dinner. I have five sisters, and our husbands and kids all line up with us, some working on the masa, some cutting rajas or cheese strips or shredding pork meat or making the guajillo sauce. Pots and pots of tamales are made. The tamales de puerco are the main dish, so we use thirty pounds of masa for those and ten pounds for each of the rajas, queso, chicken, and sweet tamales. We get all the work out of the way, as it can get hectic on Christmas Eve, when we start cooking them off around two p.m. By dinner they're all ready. Our tradition is to eat and party all evening, then open the gifts at midnight.

## COOK'S NOTE

Masa preperada is masa prepared from the store. It can be found at most Mexican grocery store that have a tortilleria inside.

1 (32-ounce) pack dried corn husks

3 pounds cushion pork meat (lean, boneless shoulder meat)

1 white onion, halved, divided

1 garlic head plus 3 garlic cloves, divided

3 dried bay leaves

2 tablespoons salt

5 dried guajillo chiles

2 dried ancho chiles

2 dried chiles de árbol

2 tablespoons chicken bouillon powder

1 tablespoon whole cumin

5 whole cloves

¼ cup pork lard

2 tablespoons all-purpose flour

### For the Masa

5 pounds prepared masa (store-bought dough, see Cook's Note)

½ cup pork lard

½ cup ice cubes

2 tablespoons salt

2 teaspoons baking powder

### For the Tomato Sauce

4 Roma tomatoes

½ white onion

2 garlic cloves

1 pickled jalapeño

1 tablespoon chicken bouillon powder

½ tablespoon dried oregano

Juice of ½ an orange

### Toppings

2 cups shredded lettuce

1 • In a large container, soak the corn husks with enough warm water to completely cover all the husks. Let the husks hydrate for 1 hour.

2 • Meanwhile, in a large pot over medium-high heat, place the pork meat and add enough water to cover. Add half an onion, the garlic head, bay leaves, and salt. Cover the pot and bring to a boil until the meat is tender, about 1½ hours. Reserve 4 cups of broth and the bay leaves for later use.

3 • Even though the masa was bought as "prepared dough," I still put a little bit of love into it. In a large bowl, combine the masa, lard, ice cubes, salt, and baking powder—this helps to make it fluffier. As my mother taught me, masa needs to be extra salty as the steam will reduce some of the saltiness. Mix the masa with your hands for about 15 minutes or until the ice melts. Cover the masa with a kitchen towel and set aside.

4 • Spoon 2 cups of the reserved pork broth into a heat-resistant bowl. Hydrate the dried guajillos, anchos, and chiles de árbol in the bowl of pork broth for 10 minutes. Transfer the chiles and their broth to a blender. Add the remaining half onion, the 3 garlic cloves, chicken bouillon powder, the reserved cooked bay leaves, the cloves, and cumin, and blend until smooth. If you don't have a high-powered blender, strain the mixture through a mesh sieve, as you don't want the texture of any unprocessed chile skins. Set aside.

5 • Make the Tomato Sauce: In a medium saucepan of boiling water, boil the tomatoes until softened, about 5 minutes. Drain and transfer to a blender. Add the onion, garlic, jalapeño, chicken bouillon, and oregano and blend until smooth. Pour the mixture into a salsa bowl and stir in the orange juice. BEAUTIFUL!!

6 • In a large stand mixer or in a large bowl with a hand blender, or using two forks, shred the pork meat and set aside. Heat a large skillet over medium-low heat, melt the lard, then stir in the flour. Cook, stirring, until creamy and lightly golden, for about 2 minutes. Add the red chili sauce and quickly stir the flour and lard mixture into the sauce, to avoid lumps. Add the 2 cups of reserved pork broth and stir until the sauce is silky smooth. Stir in the shredded meat. Now, we are ready to wrap the tamales!

7 • Drain the corn husks. Evenly spread about 2 to 3 spoonfuls of the masa dough down the center of the husk, leaving an inch on each side. Add a couple of spoonfuls of the pork filling down the center of the masa. Then securely fold the left side, then the right side of the husk over the filling. Fold the narrow bottom part up and over the seam until its nicely wrapped. Repeat with the remaining husks.

8 • Set up your tamalera (large steamer): Fill with water up to the steamer line. Stand the tamales in the steamer with the open ends facing up. Place a damp kitchen towel on top of tamales, then cover with the steamer lid (this will help keep the tamales from drying out from the top). Bring to a boil over high heat. When the water is boiling, reduce the heat to medium and cook for 1 hour 20 minutes.

9 • Turn off the heat and leave tamales in the steamer for 20 minutes to allow them to settle and firm up. If you remove them too quickly the masa is mushy and won't hold its shape when you peel off the husks.

10 • When ready to serve, remove the corn husks and top it with the lettuce and the spicy tomato sauce.

**Y LISTO AND ENJOY!**

# TAMALES DE POLLO SALSA VERDE

Prep time: 1 hour 20 minutes
Cook time: 3 hours
SERVES 10 TO 12

The second favorite tamale for our Christmas Eve feast is green salsa and chicken. They're really just as good as the pork, swapping out the green for the red salsa and chicken for pork. The green salsa is also delicious on enchiladas, short ribs, or even tossed with spaghetti in place of a red sauce.

1 (32-ounce) pack dried corn husks

3 pounds skinless, boneless chicken breast

1 white onion, halved

1 garlic head plus 3 garlic cloves, divided

1 bunch fresh cilantro, divided

1 fresh serrano chile

4 tablespoons salt, divided

8 tomatillos

3 fresh poblano peppers

2 fresh jalapeño chiles

2 tablespoons chicken bouillon powder

¼ cup pork lard

2 tablespoons cornstarch

## For the Masa

5 pounds prepared masa (store-bought dough, see Cook's Note, page 74)

½ cup pork lard

½ cup ice cubes

2 teaspoons baking powder

## Toppings

2 cups shredded lettuce

Mom's Tomato Sauce (page 180)

1 • In a large container, soak the corn husks with enough warm water to completely cover. Let the husks hydrate for 1 hour.

2 • In a large pot over high heat, bring the chicken with water to cover to a boil, half an onion, the garlic head, 4 cilantro sprigs, the serrano, and salt. Boil until the chicken is soft, about 1 hour 20 minutes. Shred the chicken and set aside. Reserve the broth.

3 • In a medium saucepan of boiling water, boil the tomatillos until they are softened, about 8 minutes. Do not let the tomatillos burst, once you see them turning brown, remove them from the heat, or they will become bitter. (If they do burst, the way to fix that bitterness is to add a little sugar.)

4 • Meanwhile, on a dry comal over medium heat, cook the poblanos and jalapeños, turning frequently, until soft, bubbling, and starting to blacken, about 5 minutes. Remove and discard the charred skin, seeds, and stems.

5 • When the tomatillos have finished cooking, drain and transfer them to a blender. Add 2 cups of the reserved chicken broth, the peppers, the remaining half onion, the 3 garlic cloves, the remaining cilantro, and the chicken bouillon powder. Blend until smooth. Set aside 1 cup of the tomatillo mixture for later use with the masa.

6 • In a large saucepan over medium heat, melt the pork lard and stir in the cornstarch until smooth. Quickly stir in the tomatillo mixture (minus the reserved cup). Add the shredded chicken and mix well. Set aside.

7 • Let's prepare the masa: Even though the masa was bought as "prepared dough," I still put a little bit of love into it. In a large bowl, combine the masa, the reserved cup of tomatillo mixture, the lard, ice cubes, salt, and baking powder—this helps to make it fluffier. As my mother taught me, masa tends to be extra salty as the steam will reduce some of the saltiness. Mix the masa with your hands for about 15 minutes or until the ice melts. Cover the masa with a kitchen towel and set aside.

8 • Drain the corn husks. Evenly spread about 2 to 3 spoonfuls of the masa dough down the center of the husk, leaving an inch on each side. Add a couple of spoonfuls of the chicken filling down the center of the masa. Then securely fold in the left side, then the right side of the husk over the filling. Fold the narrow bottom part up and over the seam until its nicely wrapped. Repeat with the remaining husks.

9 • Set up your tamalera (large steamer): Fill with water up to the steamer line. Stand the tamales in the steamer with the open ends facing up. Place a damp kitchen towel on top of the tamales, then cover with the steamer lid (this will help keep the tamales from drying out from the top). Bring to a boil over high heat. When the water is boiling, reduce the heat to medium and cook for 1 hour 20 minutes.

10 • Turn off the heat and leave the tamales in the steamer for 20 minutes to allow them to settle and firm up. If you remove them too quickly the masa is mushy and won't hold its shape when you peel off the husks.

11 • When ready to serve, remove the corn husks and top it with the lettuce and Mom's Tomato Sauce.

Y LISTO AND ENJOY!

# TAMALES DE 3 RAJAS

Prep time: 1 hour
Cook time: 1 hour 30 minutes
SERVES 10 TO 12

This is yet another tamale that shows up during our traditional Christmas gathering. Served alongside the pork and chicken versions, this one works for those who don't want meat. It's really spicy and savory. Growing up, my mom would only make it with bell peppers, cheese, and poblanos, but as we got older, us girls wanted more spice. We added jalapeños but found it wasn't spicy enough, so then we added the serrano chiles, as they always deliver the heat. When I invented this I found it to be perfect, but we make some that have only poblanos for my mother, as it's too spicy for her. It has a kick!

1 (32-ounce) pack dried corn husks

5 pounds prepared masa (store-bought dough, see Cook's Note page 74)

1 cup chicken broth (either homemade or made from 1 tablespoon chicken bouillon powder)

½ cup pork lard

½ cup ice cubes

1 tablespoon salt

2 teaspoons baking powder

8 fresh poblano peppers, seeded, deveined, and julienned

12 fresh serrano chiles, seeded, deveined, and julienned

12 fresh jalapeño chiles, seeded, deveined, and julienned

4 pounds Oaxaca cheese, shredded in long strips

Mom's Tomato Sauce (page 180), for serving

1 • In a large container, soak the corn husks with enough warm water to completely cover. Let the husks hydrate for 1 hour.

2 • Let's prepare the masa: Even though the masa was bought as "prepared dough," I still put a little bit of love into it. In a large bowl, combine the masa, chicken broth, lard, ice cubes, salt, and baking powder—this helps make it fluffier. As my mother taught me, masa needs to be extra salty as the steam will reduce some of the saltiness. Mix the masa with your hands for about 15 minutes or until the ice melts. Cover the masa with a kitchen towel and set aside.

3 • Drain the corn husks. Evenly spread about 2 to 3 spoonfuls of the masa dough down the center of the husk, leaving an inch on each side. Add strips of each pepper down the center of each husk (4 poblano strips, 4 serranos strips, and 4 jalapeño strips and a few cheese strips). Then securely fold the left side, then the right side of the husk over the filling. Fold the narrow bottom part up and over the seam until its nicely wrapped. Repeat with the remaining husks.

4 • Set up your tamalera (large steamer): Fill with water up to the steamer line. Stand the tamales in the steamer with the open ends facing up. Place a damp kitchen towel on top of the tamales, then cover with the steamer lid (this will help keep the tamales from drying out from the top). Bring to a boil over high heat. When the water is boiling, reduce the heat and cook for 1 hour 20 minutes.

5 • Turn off the heat and leave the tamales in the steamer for 20 minutes to allow them to settle and firm up. If you remove them too quickly the masa is mushy and won't hold its shape when you peel off the husks.

6 • When ready to serve, remove the corn husks and top it with Mom's Tomato Sauce.

Y LISTO AND ENJOY!

# TAMALES DE ELOTE

Prep time: 20 minutes
Cook time: 1 hour
**SERVES 10 TO 12**

These were my mom's favorite tamales when she was a little girl! In Michoacan, they're know as corundas and are wrapped in fresh corn leaves (not the husk); this is how they get their triangular shape! Depending on your mood, these tamales can be a dessert with lechera (condensed milk) or as a meal with salsa de tomatillo and crema, or with costillas de puerco en salsa roja on the side (savory)! Both very delicious! It's hard to find fresh corn leaves in the grocery stores, so to do it the Michoacan way, find a ranch or a farm where they harvest corn fields!

8 fresh white ears of corn

1 cup corn flour (maseca)

1 cup granulated sugar

7 ounces heavy cream

1 stick (8 tablespoons) unsalted butter, melted

1 tablespoon baking powder

2 tablespoons salt, divided

## Toppings

1 (13-ounce) can condensed milk (optional)

1 cup sour cream (optional)

Dad's Tomatillo Salsa (page 179, optional)

1 • Start by cutting the corn about a half inch from the bottom. Unroll and peel the husks off the cobs carefully, so that they won't tear, and discard the silk. Put the husks into a bowl filled with water to keep hydrated.

2 • Using a knife, remove the kernels from the cobs. Add the corn, in batches, to blender and blend until smooth but still slightly chunky.

3 • Transfer the blended corn masa into a large bowl. Add the flour, sugar, heavy cream, butter, sugar, baking powder, and 1 tablespoon of salt. Mix with a large spoon; the masa should be runny. Drain the corn husks from the water and pat dry.

4 • Evenly spread about 3 to 4 tablespoonfuls of the corn mixture down the center of the husk, leaving an inch on each side. Do not over fill to the top as they will fluff up and ooze out. Then securely fold in the left side, then the right side of the husk over the filling. Fold the narrow bottom part up and over the seam until its nicely wrapped. Repeat with the remaining husks.

5 • Set up your tamalera (large steamer): Fill with water up to the steamer line and add the remaining 1 tablespoon salt (to help the runny mixture set). Bring the water to a boil over high heat, then reduce the heat to medium. Stand the tamales in the steamer with the open ends facing up. Cover with the remaining fresh corn husks, creating a lid, then add a damp kitchen towel on top and cover with the steamer lid. Cook for 1 hour.

6 • You can eat these sweet or savory. Drizzle with condensed milk for sweet or with sour cream and tomatillo salsa for savory.

Y LISTO AND ENJOY!

# CHICKEN, FISH & VEGETARIAN

## Habanero Chicken Wings

## Chicken Tinga
(SHREDDED CHICKEN WITH CHIPOTLE SAUCE)

## Enchiladas de Pollo en Salsa Verde
(GREEN CHICKEN ENCHILADAS)

## Mole Rojo Pollo Estilo Nayarit
(RED MOLE CHICKEN, NAYARIT STYLE)

## Mole Negro de Pollo
(BLACK CHICKEN MOLE)

## Camarones a la Diabla
(DEVIL'S SHRIMP)

## Pescado Zarandeado Estilo Nayarit
(MEXICAN GRILLED RED SNAPPER)

## Salmon con Salsa de Mango
(GRILLED SALMON WITH MANGO SALSA)

## Mexican Quesadillas, Michoacan Style
(POTATO, GREEN PEPPER, AND BEANS-STUFFED TORTILLA DOUGH)

# HABANERO CHICKEN WINGS

Prep time: 10 minutes
Cook time: 45 minutes
SERVES 6 TO 8

4 pounds chicken wings

3 tablespoons cornstarch

1 tablespoon garlic powder

1 tablespoon smoked paprika

1 tablespoon onion powder

1 tablespoon Mesa Mia: Jenny's Favorite Seasoning

1 tablespoon freshly ground black pepper

½ cup apricot marmalade

3 fresh habanero chiles

2 garlic cloves

1 tablespoon chicken bouillon powder

2 teaspoons Maggie seasoning sauce

4 cups canola oil

French fries, for serving, optional

Wings are a guy's best friend (lol)! When we want to go a route other than Mexican food, this is one of the boys' options! But I keep upping the spice and heat level. Habanero has become my family's favorite pepper. I am surprised how much heat my younger boys can take. I have to thank my dad for this; one of the things he would do with all of his grandchildren is to introduce them to spicy early on. I feel like every guy loves chicken wings, on TikTok or Instagram—it's always a guy making wings. They're great finger food appetizers to grab when there's a game on. If my boys could, they'd order wings every single time. My daughter tells me she can eat six when we order from Wingstop, but ten when I make them. My family is not normal. We eat too much. I'd double this recipe for my family! The youngest boy is thirteen and he tries to go for third helpings. I have to stop him—you have to give your tummy time to digest and alert your brain that it's full!

1 • Start by separating the chicken wings at the joint, between the wingette and the drumette. Rinse and pat them dry. In a large bowl, combine the cornstarch, garlic powder, paprika, onion powder, seasoning, and pepper. Add the chicken and toss to coat the wings. Set aside in the refrigerator.

2 • In a blender, add the marmalade, habaneros, garlic, chicken bouillon, and Maggie sauce. Blend until smooth. Transfer the sauce to a medium saucepan over low heat and simmer until slightly thickened, about 8 minutes. Set aside.

3 • In a deep, large frying pan, heat the oil over medium heat. Check the heat by dipping a wooden spoon into the hot oil; if it sizzles, it's ready. Add the chicken pieces, 6 to 8 at a time. To achieve crispy but tender chicken wings, do not over crowd; fry until the wings are dark golden brown, 10 to 12 minutes. As you go, set the chicken aside on a rack set over a sheet pan to allow the excess oil to drain. Repeat with the remaining chicken.

4 • Transfer the fried chicken to a large bowl and drizzle the habanero sauce on top. Give them a good toss until all the chicken pieces are covered in this delicious spicy sauce. Serve with fries, if desired.

# CHICKEN TINGA

Prep time: 15 minutes
Cook time: 1 hour 20 minutes
SERVES 8

4 pounds boneless, skinless chicken breasts, each cut in half

3 medium red onions, divided

1 garlic head plus 3 garlic cloves, divided

3 dried bay leaves

1 tablespoon salt

2 cups chicken broth

2 (7-ounce) cans chipotle peppers in adobo, divided

½ cup mayonnaise

3 tablespoons chicken bouillon powder, divided

¼ cup canola oil

24 tostadas

## Toppings

½ head iceberg lettuce, shredded

Sour cream

8 ounces queso fresco

4 cups Refried Beans, warmed (page 157)

Chile de Aceite (page 174, optional)

I got part of this recipe from my friend's mom, who is from Mexico City. She cooks so well. I am always curious when someone is cooking something I like, and she didn't mind giving me the recipe. Then I combined her recipe with another recipe to make it my own. It was a hit. I use one can of chipotle in the blended sauce and a second can of whole chipotle peppers that I stir into the sauce, halving them with the spoon, so that you can have a big piece of pepper in a bite. It can be spicy, but it's my preference and it looks good to see the chunky chipotles. I like to serve these at birthday parties, served in a chafing dish and allowing everyone to do their own tostada toppings.

1 • Bring a large pot of water to a boil. Add the chicken breasts, half an onion, the garlic head split it half, the bay leaves, and salt; boil for 1 hour.

2 • While the chicken is cooking, you can thinly slice the remaining onions and prepare the toppings (shred the lettuce, crumble the queso fresco, and make the beans).

3 • When the chicken is almost done cooking, make the chipotle sauce. In a blender, add the chicken broth, 1 can of chipotles, the mayonnaise, the 3 garlic cloves, and 2 tablespoons of chicken bouillon powder. Blend until smooth; set aside.

4 • After 1 hour, remove the chicken from the pot and shred in an electric stand mixer; you don't even have to wait for the chicken to cool down. (This will save you so much time; alternatively use your fingers or forks.) Set the shredded chicken aside.

5 • In a large pan, heat the oil over medium-low heat. Add the sliced onions and the remaining 1 tablespoon of chicken bouillon powder and cook, stirring constantly, until translucent, about 3 minutes. Stir the

chicken into the onion mixture, then pour in the chipotle sauce. Add the remaining can of chipotles, leaving the peppers whole or gently cut them in half with a spoon; mix again and simmer until all the flavors have melded, 15 to 20 minutes.

6 • To serve: On a tostada, the first layer is beans, then the chicken, and top with the shredded lettuce, sour cream, queso fresco, and Chile de Aceite, if desired.

**Y LISTO AND ENJOY!**

# GREEN CHICKEN ENCHILADAS

# ENCHILADAS DE POLLO EN SALSA VERDE

Prep time: 20 minutes
Cook time: 1 hour 50 minutes
SERVES 8 TO 10

3 pounds boneless, skinless chicken breasts

1 white onion, halved, divided

1 garlic head plus 2 garlic cloves, divided

3 dried bay leaves

1 tablespoon salt

4 fresh poblano peppers

2 fresh jalapeño chiles

8 green tomatillos

1 bunch fresh cilantro

2 tablespoons chicken bouillon powder

2 cups canola oil

24 (6-inch) corn tortillas

2 cups shredded Monterey Jack cheese

## Toppings

Sour cream

Fresh cilantro, chopped

I grew up making red enchiladas, but when my daughter asked me to make green ones there was something about it that all my kids love. It's not so hot that it's overwhelming, but you still get a good kick. Using the oven to finish them off makes it so much easier, but this is an Americanized, Tex-Mex way to do it. It's a mess to do it the original way, as the tortillas sizzle in the oil after being dipped. My kids love it, as it's sort of like a quesadilla. Some people like them very over stuffed, like my husband, but my dad prefers just a little bit of filling.

1 • Bring a medium pot of water to a boil over medium-high heat. Add the chicken, half an onion, the garlic head, bay leaves, and salt. Cook until tender, about 1 hour. When the chicken has finished cooking, reserve 1 cup of the chicken broth. Shred the chicken in an electric stand mixer (or use your fingers or forks, but this is faster) and set aside.

2 • In a dry, medium comal or skillet, char the poblanos and jalapeños over medium-low heat, about 3 minutes on each side. Sweat the peppers in a plastic bag for a few minutes. Peel off the charred skin, remove the stems, devein and seed the peppers. Set aside.

3 • Bring a small saucepan of water to a boil, add the tomatillos, and cook until they are just beginning to brown, about 8 minutes. Do not let the tomatillos burst; cook just until they start to brown, then remove from the heat or they will become bitter. Drain.

(recipe continues)

4 • Transfer the peppers and the tomatillos to a blender and add the remaining 2 garlic cloves, the remaining ½ onion, cilantro, reserved 1 cup of chicken broth, and the chicken bouillon powder. Blend until smooth. Transfer the mixture to a medium, deep pan over medium-low heat, and simmer the sauce until it has slightly thickened, about 10 minutes.

5 • Preheat the oven to 350°F. Grease a (9 by 13-inch) baking dish.

6 • In a medium pan, heat the oil over medium heat. Check the heat by dipping a wooden spoon into the hot oil; if it sizzles, it's ready. Lightly fry the tortillas, one at a time, until soft, about 5 seconds on each side. Then, dip the tortillas, one at a time, in the green sauce, and place flat on a plate. Put 2 to 3 spoonfuls of the shredded chicken across the middle of the tortilla and roll it up. Repeat with the remaining tortillas. Place the enchiladas in the prepared baking dish as you go, arranged in two layers. Drizzle the remaining sauce and then sprinkle the cheese over the top. Bake until cheese melts, 25 to 30 minutes. Serve topped with sour cream and cilantro.

**Y LISTO AND ENJOY!**

## RED MOLE CHICKEN, NAYARIT STYLE

# MOLE ROJO POLLO ESTILO NAYARIT

Prep time: 45 minutes
Cook time: 1 hour 35 minutes
SERVES 8 TO 10

1 (5-pound) whole chicken

2 white onions, divided

1 garlic head plus 3 garlic cloves, divided

3 dried bay leaves

1 tablespoon salt

8 dried guajillo chiles

6 dried chiles de árbol

1 tablespoon canola oil

3 Roma tomatoes, halved

4 whole allspice

1 tablespoon cumin seeds

1 tablespoon dried oregano

1 tablespoon freshly ground black pepper

2 tablespoons chicken bouillon powder

1 cup corn flour (maseca)

2 tablespoons pork lard

**Toppings**

1 white onion, thinly sliced into rounds

Juice of 2 fresh limes

**Serve with**

Preferred rice

Refried Beans (page 157)

Warm tortillas

The base of this recipe comes from my husband's family, from Nayarit. I made it my own by swapping in different chiles. Instead of using New Mexico chiles I add guajillo chiles, which have a little bit of a dried fruit aroma; ancho chiles, which have a sweeter taste almost like a dried prune; as well as a bit of spice from the chile de árbol. I actually prefer it spicier than this, and use twelve or thirteen chile de árbol instead of six when making it for my family. But unless you're truly used to that level of heat, be cautious!

1 • Cut the chicken breasts, through the bones, into thirds.

2 • In a large pot over medium-high heat, bring to a boil the chicken pieces with water to cover, half an onion, the garlic head, bay leaves, and salt. Cook, covered, until the meat is very soft and tender, 1 hour 20 minutes.

3 • While the chicken is cooking, devein and remove the seeds from the guajillos. In a dry cast-iron skillet over medium heat, toast the guajillos, turning frequently, until they start to bubble, 2 to 3 minutes. (It's very important not to char the chiles as they will become bitter.) Set aside. In the same skillet, toast the chiles de árbol, turning constantly as they burn more easily, until they begin to darken, 2 to 3 minutes. In a medium bowl, combine 2 cups of chicken broth from the pot and add the chiles to rehydrate for 10 minutes.

(recipe continues on page 93)

4 • In the same skillet over medium heat, heat the oil and add the tomatoes, the remaining ½ onion cut into quarters, and the 3 garlic cloves. Cook, stirring frequently, until the tomatoes are soft, about 8 minutes. Add the rehydrated chiles, the allspice, and cumin, and simmer, stirring frequently, about 5 minutes. Transfer everything in the skillet to a blender, add the oregano, black pepper, and chicken bouillon powder. Set aside.

5 • In a dry comal over high heat, toast the corn flour, stirring constantly, until golden brown, about 2 minutes. To prevent it from burning, do not stop stirring. Transfer the toasted corn flour to the blender with the other ingredients and blend until smooth. If you do not have a high-powered blender, strain the chile sauce through a fine-mesh strainer.

6 • When cooked, remove the chicken and broth from the pot and set aside. In the same pot, melt the lard over medium heat. Add the mole sauce; mix well and add 2 cups of broth. Add more broth until you achieve your desired thickness. Add the chicken back to the pot and simmer for 15 minutes.

7 • Place the thinly sliced onions in a shallow bowl and toss them with the lime juice. Serve the mole garnished with the lime-pickled onions, rice, Refried Beans, and warm tortillas.

Y LISTO AND ENJOY!

# MOLE NEGRO DE POLLO

Prep time: 45 minutes
Cook time: 1 hour 30 minutes
SERVES 8 TO 10

Oaxaca is known for mole, including mole negro, but this version is from Michoacan where my mother grew up. The unique technique involves charring—to the point of burning—the seeds and lightly charring the bolillo to create the black color and depth of flavor in the dish. When I first saw my grandmother cook the seeds to the point where they flame up, I thought there's no way that is going to taste good, it will be so bitter. But to my surprise, the other seasonings and the sweetness of the chocolate perfectly balance out the bitterness. Some people char tortillas in place of the bolillo, but my family prefers bolillo as we feel it really adds to the texture and it definitely has a slightly different flavor. As with birria (see page 130), moles are often made in big quantities for events like weddings or baptisms.

- 1 (3-pound) whole chicken, cut into 10 pieces, cutting breasts in half
- ½ white onion
- 1 garlic head plus 4 garlic cloves, divided
- 3 dried bay leaves
- 1 tablespoon salt
- 3 dried ancho chiles
- 2 dried pasilla chiles
- 2 dried guajillo chiles
- 1 cup pork lard
- 1 (3.1-ounce) dark chocolate bar (I like to use Abuelita chocolate)
- ½ cup roasted peanuts
- ½ cup raw pecans
- ½ cup raw almonds
- ½ cup black raisins
- ½ cup sesame seeds, plus more for garnish
- 1 cinnamon stick, broken into pieces
- 1 tablespoon dried oregano
- 5 whole allspice
- 1 bolillo
- 2 tablespoons chicken bouillon powder
- Mexican Red Rice (page 146) and beans

1 • In a large pot over medium-high heat, cook the chicken with water to cover, the onion, garlic head, bay leaves, and salt; bring to a boil, then cover the pot and cook until the meat is soft and tender, about 1 hour 20 minutes. When cooked, set the chicken aside and reserve the broth.

2 • Meanwhile, devein and remove the seeds from the anchos, pasillas, and guajillos, but do not throw away the seeds. Butterfly the pods and toast them on a dry comal or skillet over medium heat, until they begin to bubble, about 1 minute on each side. Set aside.

3 • In a clay pot or large skillet over medium heat, melt the lard. Add the chocolate, peanuts, pecans, almonds, raisins, sesame seeds, cinnamon stick, the 4 garlic cloves, oregano, and allspice. Mix well and cook, stirring, until toasted, about 5 minutes. Pour into a blender.

4 • On a dry a comal or skillet over medium heat, toast the bolillo until slightly burnt on the outside crust. Add it to the blender.

5 • Next, add the seeds (reserved from the chile pods) to the hot, dry comal over high heat. Stirring constantly, toast the seeds and allow them to completely blacken and burn. Continue heating until you create a flame (as soon as you see the flame turn off the heat!). BEAUTIFUL!!! Transfer the seeds to a small bowl, and add 1 cup of the reserved chicken broth to quickly rehydrate them, about 1 minute. Add the seeds and their broth to the blender.

6 • Add an additional cup of reserved chicken broth to the blender with the nuts, the chicken bouillon powder, and bolillo; blend until smooth. Transfer the mole sauce to a clay pot or a large saucepan, and simmer over medium-low heat, about 10 minutes. Add the chicken pieces. Now, it's ready to serve.

7 • Serve with Mexican Red Rice and beans, and sprinkle more sesame seeds on top of the mole to garnish.

Y LISTO AND ENJOY!

## DEVIL'S SHRIMP

# CAMARONES A LA DiABLA

**Prep time: 10 minutes**
**Cook time: 13 minutes**

**SERVES 8 TO 10**

4 pounds (30/40) shrimp, shell on

4 Roma tomatoes

20 dried chiles de árbol

½ white onion

¼ cup mayonnaise

¼ cup sour cream

2 tablespoons chicken bouillon powder

4 garlic cloves (2 whole, 2 minced), divided

Juice of 1 fresh orange

Juice of 1 fresh lime

¼ cup canola oil

### For Serving

Preferred rice

4 fresh limes, cut into wedges

1 (16-ounce) box saltine crackers

A la diabla because it's super fiery! Like you're in hell! After all, we use twenty chile de árbol. My older sister Reyna's husband's family ate this, and when she first introduced me to it, I said I think you're missing the heat. His family didn't like it too spicy. Needless to say, I brought it back to its origins. Keep the shrimp shell on, as that's where the flavor comes from.

Most of us love the heat but none more than my sister Gloria. We go to restaurants and it's never spicy enough. In fact, restaurants have had her sign a release saying that they are not responsible for what happens when she asks them to increase the heat to more and more spicy! When she was a little girl, she'd eat five of the canned jalapeños on one tortilla. Some things never change!

### COOK'S NOTE

Remember to strain the sauce through a fine-mesh strainer if you do not have a high-powered blender.

1 • Rinse the shrimp and pat them dry. Set aside.

2 • In a small saucepan, bring 3 cups of water to a boil over high heat. Add the tomatoes and chiles de árbol and boil until softened, 8 to 10 minutes. Transfer the tomatoes, chiles, and water to a blender. Add the onion, mayonnaise, sour cream, chicken bouillon powder, the 2 whole garlic cloves, the orange juice, and lime juice. Blend until smooth. (See Cook's Note.) Set aside.

3 • In a large pan or wok, heat the oil over medium heat. Add the shrimp and 2 minced garlic cloves and cook, stirring constantly, until the shrimp are pink, about 3 minutes. Add the spicy sauce and simmer until flavors have melded, for 10 minutes. Serve with rice, limes, and saltine crackers.

**Y LISTO AND ENJOY!**

## MEXICAN GRILLED RED SNAPPER

# PESCADO ZARANDEADO ESTILO NAYARIT

Prep time: 5 minutes
Cook time: 15 minutes

**SERVES 4 TO 6**

1 (3- to 4-pound) whole red snapper

2 tablespoons mayonnaise

2 tablespoons yellow mustard

Juice of 1 fresh lime

1 tablespoon salt

1 tablespoon freshly ground black pepper

4 tablespoons salsa Huichol, or Tapatio, hot sauce

### For Serving

Cilantro Lime Rice (page 149)

Refried Beans (page 157)

Salsa Tatemada de Molcajete (page 177)

### Equipment

Folding grilling basket

Nayarit, where my husband's family is from, is on the coast, so they have all this great seafood. This recipe is true to the region, simply cooked in a grilling basket, and served with the regional favorite, salsa Huichol, a hot sauce.

1 • Heat a grill to medium heat.

2 • Rinse the fish and pat dry. With a sharp knife, make a slit from head to tail to butterfly the fish, so that it opens like a book. In a small bowl, combine the mayonnaise, mustard, and lime juice. Coat the fish with the mixture. Season the fish inside and out with the salt and pepper. Then drizzle the inside of the fish with the salsa Huichol.

3 • Place the fish in a grilling basket and put it on the grill; grill until crispy, about 10 minutes, then flip and grill until the other side is crispy, about 5 minutes. Remove the fish from the grilling basket and serve it on a large platter with Cilantro Lime Rice, Refried Beans, and Salsa Tatemada de Molcajete.

**Y LISTO AND ENJOY!**

# SALMON CON SALSA DE MANGO

GRILLED SALMON WITH MANGO SALSA

Prep time: 30 minutes
Cook time: 6 minutes

SERVES 4 TO 6

1 (5-pound) slab of salmon (skin on), cut into 5 portions

2 tablespoons garlic powder

2 tablespoons freshly ground black pepper

½ cup teriyaki sauce

2 tablespoons minced garlic

1 tablespoon light brown sugar

1 tablespoon Dijon mustard

Pinch chile de árbol pepper flakes, toasted

## For The Mango Salsa

2 mangos, cut into ½-inch cubes

2 small cucumbers, diced

½ medium red onion, diced

½ bunch fresh cilantro, chopped

2 fresh habanero chiles, stemmed and minced

1 tablespoon minced garlic

Apple cider vinegar

Juice of ½ fresh lime

Olive oil spray, for the grill

## For Serving

Cilantro Lime Rice (page 149, optional)

Grilled asparagus (optional)

My family generally loves salmon any way we prepare it, but there was a time when my boys were little and still making faces about eating fish. This recipe was how I won them over. Adding mango salsa hid the fishy flavor of the salmon, and the combination is sweet and tangy with cilantro and onion. I never expected sweet mango and savory fish to go so well together! Big tip on cooking salmon, make sure the grill is hot and the grates are clean to ensure that the fish won't stick.

1 • Season the salmon on all sides with garlic powder and black pepper. In a medium bowl, combine the teriyaki sauce, minced garlic, brown sugar, mustard, and pepper flakes. Drizzle the sauce over the salmon and allow the fish to marinate for 15 minutes.

2 • Make the Mango Salsa: In a medium bowl, toss together the mangos, cucumbers, onion, cilantro, habaneros, minced garlic, a splash of vinegar, and the lime juice. Set aside.

3 • Heat grill to high and grease the grate with oil spray. Grill salmon flesh side down, with the thickest part nearest to you for ease of flipping. Grill until it begins to turn pink in the middle, about 3 minutes. Then, using a large, flat spatula, quickly flip. Cook until it is no longer raw in the middle, an about 3 minutes, or until cooked to your liking.

4 • Serve with the  salsa. and Cilantro Lime Rice and grilled asparagus, if desired!

# MEXICAN QUESADILLAS,

POTATO, GREEN PEPPER AND BEANS-STUFFED TORTILLA DOUGH

## MICHOACAN STYLE

Prep time: 45 minutes
Cook time: 1 hour 20 minutes
SERVES 6 TO 8

Why are these called quesadillas if they have no cheese? I'll be honest, I am not sure—it may just be a Michoacan thing. My mother says, you can add cheese on top, if you like. Day-old refried beans work really well here, as you don't want the stuffing to be too saucy. If you make the beans on the same day that you're making these, make the beans first thing so that they have some time to firm up a bit.

### For the Masa

4 cups corn flour (maseca)

1 cup all-purpose flour

4 cups warm water

3 tablespoons pork lard

2 cups cooked pinto beans (see page 158, I also like Peruvian beans)

4 tablespoons plus 4 cups canola oil, divided

2 Russet potatoes, peeled and diced

1 beefsteak tomato, diced

½ white onion, diced

½ tablespoon salt

2 green bell peppers, julienned

1 (8-ounce) Monterey cheese block, cut in 2-inch strips

### To Serve

Shredded lettuce

Sour cream

Salsa

### Equipment

Tortilla press

Thin plastic bag, cut open so it can fold

1 • Let's start by making the masa: In a medium bowl, mix the corn flour, all-purpose flour, and warm water. Knead the dough until smooth, about 5 minutes. Cover the dough with a damp kitchen towel and set aside. (This will prevent the masa from drying out.)

2 • In a medium pan, heat lard over medium heat. It's very important to allow the lard to get quite hot, then turn off the burner before adding the beans. This prevents everything from going up in flames! Add the beans to the pan and cover the pot quickly with a pot lid to prevent the fat from splattering on your stovetop (or you!). Turn the heat to medium-low and bring the mixture to a simmer; mash it up as it bubbles. An immersion blender can help you do this more quickly. Hand mashing to can be dangerous as it can burn when it bubbles. Set aside.

3 • In a medium pan over medium heat, heat 4 tablespoons of oil; add the potatoes and cook, stirring frequently, until golden brown, 15 to 20 minutes. Stir in the tomato, onion, and salt. Set aside.

4 • Divide the three fillings (beans, potatoes, and green bell peppers with cheese) into equal parts, to have equal amounts of the three types of fried quesadillas.

5 • On a tortilla press, cover both sides of the press with a thin plastic bag, to prevent the dough from sticking. Roll a small handful of the masa into a 2- to 3-inch ball. Place the dough ball in the center of the tortilla press and gently press down to shape it into a 5 to 6-inch soft tortilla.

6 • Add the desired filling to the middle of the tortilla, and gently fold and press all the edges to secure the filling inside. It should look like a sealed, stuffed soft taco. Repeat with the remaining dough and fillings.

7 • In a medium skillet, heat 2 cups of oil over medium heat. Check the heat by dipping a wooden spoon into the hot oil; if it sizzles, it's ready. Fry the quesadillas until golden brown, about 3 minutes on each side. Drain and serve. Repeat with remaining the quesadillas.

8 • Top it with shredded lettuce, a drizzle of sour cream, and your preferred salsa and enjoy. Beautiful!

Y LISTO AND ENJOY!

# PORK & BEEF

## Carnitas
(SLOW COOKED FRIED PORK)

## Manchamantel
(FRIED PORK
IN DARK CHILI SAUCE)

## Costillitas en Salsa Verde
(PORK SHORT RIBS IN GREEN SAUCE)

## Gorditas de Queso con Chorizo
(CHEESE AND CHORIZO
FRIED TORTILLAS)

## Chiles en Nogada
(BEEF-STUFFED POBLANOS
IN WALNUT SAUCE)

## Tostadas de Deshebrada
(SHREDDED BEEF TOSTADAS)

## Bistec Ranchero
(RANCHERO BEEF SKIRT STEAK)

## Enchiladas de Carne Molida en Chile Rojo
(RED CHILE BEEF ENCHILADAS)

## SLOW COOKED FRIED PORK

# CARNITAS

**Prep time: 15 minutes**
**Cook time: 2 hours 30 minutes**
**SERVES 8 TO 10**

5 cups pork lard

4 pounds boneless pork shoulder butt roast, cut into 4-inch cubes

1¼ white onions, divided

1 garlic head plus 3 garlic cloves, divided

3 dried bay leaves

1 pound pork short ribs

2 tablespoons salt

1 (12-ounce) can Coca-Cola

1 fresh orange, juice and peel

### For Serving

1 white onion, diced

1 bunch fresh cilantro, chopped

Salsa Cruda (page 173)

6 limes, cut into wedges

Warm (6-inch) tortillas or rice and beans

When I think of carnitas, I return to childhood memories of my dad's friend cooking outside over a wood fire and using a great big copper or aluminum pot called a cazo. It was special, not something you had normally because it takes too long to make. I honestly don't know how he did it, how did they adjust the flame of the fire under the pot? He would add every piece of the pig to that cazo, ears, pickled pork skin—an entire pig! Big old wooden spoons were used to stir the pork. All my dad's friends and my uncles gathered around the pot, telling jokes and sharing stories, having a beer, while the women would sit at the table eating properly.

Carnitas, cueritos, and buche were eaten as appetizers served with hot sauce and lime juice. For me it was like a delicacy. Only a person who knew how to make it would own a cazo. The meat can actually dry out during the cooking, so as simple as it seems, there is a strategy and method you must know. I recommend getting a marbleized pork roast, not too lean. You want marbled fat for flavor. By mixing in the short ribs, you get the color and richness that's correct; the bone gives it the flavor.

1 • In a large, deep cast-iron pot, melt the lard over high heat. Once lard is very hot, carefully add the pork shoulder pieces with the whole onion cut in half, the garlic head cut in half horizontally, and the bay leaves. Sear the meat to seal, turning occasionally, until golden brown on all sides, about 30 minutes. When the lard reaches a boiling point again, after about 30 minutes, add the short ribs. Fry until the ribs are golden brown, about 10 minutes.

2 • In a blender, combine the remaining ¼ onion, the 3 garlic cloves, the cooked bay leaves, garlic head, and onion. Add the salt and ¼ cup of water. Blend until smooth.

3 • Add the blended ingredients, the can of Coke, the orange juice, and orange peel to the pot and stir. Cover the pot securely (sometimes I add foil as well) and reduce the heat to low. Continue frying over low heat until all is tender, about 2 hours, stirring every 30 minutes with a wooden spoon to prevent sticking and burning; the meat should be fall-apart tender!

4 • Top the carnitas off with onions, cilantro, and Salsa Cruda, and squeeze lime juice all over. Serve with tortillas as tacos or with rice and beans as a side dish.

**Y LISTO AND ENJOY!**

# MANCHAMANTEL

**Prep time: 45 minutes**
**Cook time: 1 hour 10 minutes**
**SERVES 8 TO 10**

This one got its name because it's kind of like a dark mole. It translates: you're going to stain your tablecloth! That's exactly what happens when you have mole—and that's why Mexican tables are often covered with plastic linens! Back in the day, my mom used to do that because with all those red sauces we served in a normal week we'd get the sauce everywhere. This recipe is pork short ribs in a mole-like sauce and it has a million spices. All the ingredients make it look intimidating but you will get on a roll, and once you're done and have tasted it, you'll think, "Huh, this wasn't so bad!"

4 pounds pork flanken short ribs

1 cup pork lard

2 dried bay leaves

1 tablespoon salt

8 dried California chiles

2 dried pasilla chiles

6 dried chiles de árbol

4 cups hot water

1 (3.1-ounce) dark chocolate bar (I like to use Abuelita chocolate)

½ cup raw almonds

½ cup pumpkin seeds (shelled)

½ cup sesame seeds

2 dried prunes

6 garlic cloves

½ cinnamon stick

1 teaspoon whole peppercorns

1 teaspoon whole allspice

1 teaspoon whole cumin seeds

½ cup (1-inch cubed) peeled apple

1 plantain, peeled and sliced

½ white onion, halved

2 Roma tomatoes, halved

½ cup (1-inch cubed) pineapple

1 small Mexican Bolillo, cut into 1-inch cubes (page 43)

6 saltine cracker squares

1 (6-inch) corn tortilla

2 tablespoons chicken bouillon powder

Juice of 2 fresh oranges

## For Serving

Mexican Red Rice (page 146)

Warm 6-inch corn tortillas

1 • Rinse the meat and pat dry. Cut the short rib slabs between the bones to separate them. Melt the lard in a disco (Mexican frying pan) over medium-high heat. Check the heat by dipping a wooden spoon into the hot oil; if it sizzles, it's ready. Carefully add the short ribs, bay leaves, and salt and fry until crispy, about 30 minutes. Remove the meat using tongs and set aside in a bowl or pot, leaving a cup of fat in the disco to fry the chiles and the rest of the ingredients.

2 • Devein and seed the California and pasilla chiles but leave the chiles de árbol whole. Reduce the heat under the disco to medium-low. Add all the chiles to the disco and lightly fry them, about 5 minutes. Remove the chiles from the fat and place them into a large bowl with the hot water. Add the chocolate bar and set aside to allow the chiles to hydrate and the chocolate to soften.

3 • In the same disco, fry the almonds, pumpkin seeds, sesame seeds, prunes, garlic, cinnamon stick, peppercorns, allspice, and cumin seeds until toasted, about 5 minutes. BEAUTIFUL! Remove the fried ingredients and place in the same bowl with the chiles to hydrate.

4 • Now repeat the process, fry the apple, plantain, onion, tomatoes, and pineapple until softened, about 5 minutes (add more lard if needed). Transfer them all to the bowl as well. Finally, fry the bolillo, crackers, and tortilla until golden brown and crispy, about 5 minutes, being careful not to burn them, and set aside. Do not add this batch to the bowl of water.

5 • Transfer everything from the bowl, including the water, to a blender, and add the chicken bouillon powder. Blend until smooth, then add the bolillo, crackers, and tortilla and blend again. (Make in batches if needed, and there's no need to strain if using high-powered blender.)

6 • Return the ribs to the disco over medium heat and immediately stir in the sauce and orange juice. Add 1 cup of water to the blender and pulse it to collect the sauce left behind. Add this to the pan as well. Simmer until tender, about 20 minutes. Serve with Mexican Red Rice and warm tortillas.

**Y LISTO AND ENJOY!**

# PORK SHORT RIBS IN GREEN SAUCE

# COSTILLITAS EN SALSA VERDE

Prep time: 30 minutes
Cook time: 1 hour 20 minutes

**SERVES 8 TO 10**

3 pounds pork flanken short ribs (see Cook's Note)

2 white onions, divided

6 garlic cloves, divided

3 dried bay leaves

6 whole peppercorns

1 tablespoon salt

2 tablespoons lard

4 Russet potatoes, peeled and quartered

8 green tomatillos

6 fresh serrano chiles

½ bunch fresh cilantro

2 tablespoons chicken bouillon powder

## For Serving

White rice

Warm 6-inch corn tortillas

This is by far my son Joshua's favorite meal. He even learned to make it at the age of eleven—we have it on video. This is everyone's favorite pork stew and is something you can find at pretty much every authentic Mexican restaurant. It's another recipe that a lot of my followers say takes them back to childhood or when their grandmother was alive. We call it Costillitas because it's super small pieces of rib that are cut from flanken-style strips of short ribs. That cut of rib is so popular now, you can find them at Costco.

## COOK'S NOTE

Flanken short ribs are cut across the bone in connected strips.

1 • Cut between the bone and the meat to separate the short ribs into pieces. In a large Dutch oven or medium pot, bring the ribs, in water to cover, to a boil, then reduce the heat to medium and add half an onion, 3 garlic cloves, the bay leaves, peppercorns, and salt; cover and cook until soft, about 30 minutes. Remove the ribs from the water and pat dry.

2 • Thinly slice 1 onion and set aside. Heat the lard in a large skillet over medium heat, and fry the short ribs until browned, about 15 minutes. Add the sliced onion and the potatoes and cook, stirring frequently, until the potatoes are browned but not cooked through, about 10 minutes.

3 • Next, heat a medium dry comal or skillet over medium-low heat, and roast the tomatillos, serranos, the remaining ½ onion cut into wedges, and the remaining 3 garlic cloves until the chiles are lightly charred, about 10 minutes. Place all in blender, add the cilantro and chicken bouillon powder and blend until smooth. BEAUTIFUL! Immediately pour the sauce over the ribs and simmer until tender, 15 to 20 minutes. Serve with white rice and warm tortillas.

**Y LISTO AND ENJOY!**

# GORDITAS DE QUESO CON CHORIZO

**Prep time: 30 minutes**
**Cook time: 20 minutes**
**SERVES 8 TO 10**

Similar to pupusas, these are made using fresh masa. It's sort of like stretching out a tortilla, but the masa is only about three inches wide. Gorditas are meant to be "fat," that's how they get their name. They are really fast to make, and the chorizo is also fast to cook. We stuff it with cheese as well, because my kids love it. You use almost the same process as making Mexican quesadillas but the stuffing and shape is different. They're very popular for breakfast. If I don't have any eggs this is what I'll make. I grab my flour and in less than twenty minutes I am already cooking them. The masa just needs warm water and you don't have to let it sit. You form like small corn tortillas and you close them sort of like dumplings, pressing to seal them with the palm of your hand so the stuffing doesn't ooze out. Shallow fried on the comal or toasted, they take about five minutes each to be ready.

These are fun for kids to do, too, as it's sort of like clay for them. I can tell which of my nieces is going to like to cook by watching them play with regular clay, because, like I did when I was a little girl, they form food with the clay. Cooking these with me, they learn and have fun at the same time. As early as eight years old, my mom was making gorditas for her family. She had eighteen brothers, and she was the oldest child. Her mother was always pregnant, so my mom had to learn really quickly how to feed her baby brothers. They would have gorditas with just salt most of the time. If they had cheese, it would be like a feast and they were in heaven. She had to make her own masa unsupervised, stoke the fire with the logs, and she says she sometimes burned her hair! But she raised her younger siblings, and they saw her as a mom.

2 cups corn flour
(maseca)

2 cups warm water

1 teaspoon salt

2 pounds pork chorizo

Canola oil, if needed

2 pounds Oaxaca cheese,
shredded

**Toppings**

Shredded lettuce

Cotija cheese, crumbled

Sour cream

Salsa Taquera (page 170)

1 • In a medium bowl, combine the corn flour, water, and salt, and mix with your hands to get the best results. Knead until it is not sticky, about 5 minutes, then cover the bowl with a damp kitchen towel to prevent the dough from drying out.

2 • In a medium skillet over medium heat, cook the chorizo, stirring frequently, until browned, 8 to 10 minutes. Remove the chorizo from the oil and set aside. Reserve the chorizo oil.

3 • Heat the reserved chorizo oil on a large comal or skillet over medium-low heat. (Use a bit of canola oil if you need to supplement the amount.)

4 • Form the masa into 2- to 3-inch dough balls. Stretch the dough balls out to 5 inches, and place 1 tablespoon of Oaxaca cheese and 1 tablespoon of chorizo in the middle. Close the dough with your fingers, forming a ball around the filling, then press and flatten it into the shape of a gordita.

5 • Add the gorditas to the oil as soon as you finish forming them to prevent drying. By doing this, not only are they going to get the red chorizo color, but the masa will have extra chorizo flavor as well. Cook until they are puffy, with a golden-brown crust, 3 to 5 minutes on each side. Open each gordita with a knife and stuff with shredded lettuce, Cotija cheese, a drizzle of sour cream, and Salsa Taquera.

**Y LISTO AND ENJOY!**

# BEEF-STUFFED POBLANO IN WALNUT SAUCE

# CHILES EN NOGADA

**Prep time: 20 minutes**
**Cook time: 1 hour 15 minutes**
**SERVES 8**

These are sort of like chile rellenos, but people battle over whether they should be covered in egg batter. As it's covered in a creamy white sauce that has so many good ingredients, like fresh apples, peaches, and pears, I don't think an egg batter adds anything to dish. There's a lot of cutting and chopping to just stuff a pepper, but at the end of the day it is so worth the trouble. The sweet and spicy picadillo-like filling is fruity and nutty rather than just veggie flavored. But the secret is in the sauce, it will make it or kill it. I've seen many people use pecans instead of walnuts or almonds, but I think that makes it too sweet. Leaving the stem on the chile pod creates an elegant look that's rustic at the same time. It's a showstopper at the holidays. Depending on your source, it was either a group of Augustinian nuns or three girlfriends of Trigarante Army soldiers who created the original Chiles en Nogada in Puebla in the 1820s. But either way, it celebrates Mexican history—and is popular around Mexican Independence Day, as the colors of the Mexican flag are featured in the garnish of green cilantro and red pomegranate seeds over the white sauce.

6 tablespoons canola oil, divided

½ white onion, diced

2 garlic cloves, minced

1 pound (80/20) ground beef

1 pound ground pork

½ cup sherry cooking wine (or brandy or whiskey), divided

1 teaspoon salt

1 teaspoon ground dried oregano

1 teaspoon ground cinnamon

½ teaspoon ground cloves

3 Roma tomatoes

¼ cup chopped green olives

2 cups sliced raw almonds, divided

1 apple, diced

1 peach, diced

1 green pear, diced

1 cup pine nuts

½ cup apple cider vinegar

½ cup golden raisins

1 ripe plantain, diced

8 fresh poblano chiles (roasted, peeled, and seeded)

1½ cups whole milk

8 ounces goat cheese (or cream cheese)

1 cup walnuts

1 tablespoon chicken bouillon powder

1 bunch fresh cilantro, coarsely chopped

2 pomegranates, seeded

(recipe continues on page 119)

1 • Heat 2 tablespoons of oil in a medium skillet over medium heat. Add the onion and cook, stirring frequently, until it begins to become translucent, about 3 minutes, then add the garlic and cook, stirring frequently, until aromatic, about 2 minutes. Add the ground beef and the ground pork and cook, stirring frequently, until browned, about 10 minutes. Stir in ½ cup of sherry, and season with the salt, oregano, cinnamon, and cloves.

2 • In a blender, puree the tomatoes and pour over the meat. Cover the skillet and simmer until the liquid has reduced completely, about 8 minutes. Add the olives, 1 cup water, and 1 cup of almonds and bring the mixture to a simmer again until completely reduced, 10 to 12 minutes.

3 • Heat 2 tablespoons of oil in a separate medium skillet over medium heat. Add the apple, peach, and pear and cook, stirring frequently, until golden brown, 6 to 8 minutes. Drain the oil from the fruit and transfer the fruit to the ground beef skillet. Stir in the pine nuts and the vinegar. Add the raisins, cover the skillet, and simmer over medium heat until the fruit and raisins are soft, 5 to 7 minutes. There should be no liquid remaining in the meat mixture. Set aside. In a separate medium skillet, heat the remaining 2 tablespoons of oil over medium-high heat, and fry the plantains until

golden brown, about 5 minutes. Stir the plantains into the meat mixture. Set aside.

4 • Heat a large comal or skillet over medium-high heat. Cook the poblanos, turning occasionally, until charred on all sides, 2 to 3 minutes. (Alternatively, char the chiles on the stovetop directly over a low open flame.) Do not over roast, as you want them to remain firm enough for stuffing. Put the poblanos in a gallon-size, resealable plastic bag; allow to sweat for 10 minutes to help loosen the skin. Peel away the charred layer of skin. Slice them lengthwise on one side to open a pocket and remove the seeds. Keep the stems intact. Stuff the poblanos with the ground beef mixture.

5 • To a blender, add the milk, goat cheese, the remaining 1 cup of almonds, the remaining ¼ cup of sherry, the walnuts, and the chicken bouillon powder and blend until smooth.

6 • Serve the stuffed chiles on a platter and cover the poblanos with the nut sauce, then garnish with the cilantro on the stem ends and the pomegranate seeds on the tip ends, to simulate the Mexican flag.

**Y LISTO AND ENJOY!**

# SHREDDED BEEF TOSTADAS

# T⊙STADAS DE DESHEBRADA

Prep time: 45 minutes
Cook time: 2 hours

SERVES 8 TO 10

**3 pounds beef flank roast** (thick cut and lean)

½ white onion

1 garlic head

3 dried bay leaves

6 whole black peppercorns

2 tablespoons salt

24 (6-inch) corn tostadas

## For the Escabeche (Pickled vegetables)

1 medium red onion, thinly sliced

1 medium carrot, shredded

1 fresh manzano chile (apple pepper), julienned (see Cook's Note)

Juice of 1 fresh lime

1 teaspoon salt

1 teaspoon dried oregano

## Toppings

Refried Beans (page 157)

½ medium head iceberg lettuce

Mom's Tomato Sauce (page 180)

Sour cream

Cotija cheese, crumbled

My parents would make this when my dad had made some extra money, and we knew if we had this type of meat in this amount in the house it meant we were celebrating something. You can serve these for kids' birthday parties or family gatherings. You've got packets of tostadas, a big pot of meat shredded into thick pieces, refried beans, sour cream, and shredded lettuce that look so pretty on display for serving. Building your own tostadas is so much fun, plus kids are picky so they can do it their way, and young moms with babies will just put some cheese or refried beans on their tostadas. But if you go all in, with different salsas and all the toppings, you can end up with a heavy, four-inch-high tostada. It will fall apart when you take a bite and be a mess, but you won't care. Just close your eyes, the chiles might splatter on your face!

## COOK'S NOTE

Manzanos chiles are known in English as apple peppers, and are sweet and spicy, like habaneros.

1 • In a tall pot, cover the flank roast with water. Add ½ the white onion, the garlic, bay leaves, peppercorns, and salt; cover and cook for 30 minutes over high heat, then reduce to medium-low heat and cook, still covered, until the meat is very tender, about 1½ hours. This is how I check if meat is ready: with your fingers or tongs, pull meat away from the roast and if it easily shreds off (pulls apart), it's ready. Remove from pot and set aside to cool down before shredding the meat by hand. Set aside.

2 • While the meat is cooking, make the escabeche: Arrange the red onion, carrot, and chile on a flat serving dish and squeeze the lime juice all over them. Season with the salt and oregano. Toss gently and set aside.

3 • Now, let's build the tostadas. Spread 2 tablespoons of beans on the tostada, add 3 hefty spoonfuls of beef, a handful of lettuce, some escabeche, drizzle with the tomato sauce and sour cream, and top it all with some Cotija cheese.

**Y LISTO AND ENJOY!**

# BiSTEC RANCHERO◉

Prep time: 15 minutes
Cook time: 45 minutes
SERVES 6 TO 8

2 pounds beef skirt steak

2 tablespoons pork lard (manteca)

2 tablespoons chicken bouillon powder, divided

1 tablespoon cornstarch

3 garlic cloves, shaved, divided

1½ white onion, sliced

½ cup canola oil

2 Russet potatoes, peeled wedges

3 Roma tomatoes, sliced into wedges

2 fresh jalapeño chiles, julienned

2 fresh serrano chiles, julienned, divided

1 bunch fresh cilantro, roughly chopped

## For Serving

Preferred rice

Refried Beans (page 157)

This is a recipe for one of those days when you need something quick and you go into the fridge and say what do I have? Back in the day, skirt steak was one of the most inexpensive cuts of meat and we always had it in the fridge. Other kitchen staples are the Mexican colors—red tomato, white onions, and green jalapeños. With those ingredients, you know you will have a quick meal. I added the potato recently, but if you're a multi-tasker like me, and can cook the elements all at once, you can still get it done pretty quickly. Serve this for breakfast in a salsa with eggs on the side, or with rice and beans for dinner. Almost always, I opt for rice and beans, and I just change up the rice flavor to keep it interesting—red rice or rice with corn, or Cilantro Lime Rice (page 149). Get creative!

1 • Start by cutting the steak into thin (2-inch-long) strips. Set aside.

2 • Heat the lard in a large pan over medium heat. Add the meat, and sprinkle in 1 tablespoon of chicken bouillon powder and the cornstarch and cook, stirring constantly, until the meat has browned and released its juices, about 5 minutes. Add 2 cloves of shaved garlic and 1 whole sliced onion and mix until all is combined; cover and cook until the meat's juices have been reabsorbed, about 10 minutes.

3 • Meanwhile, in a separate medium skillet over medium-high heat, heat the canola oil. Check the heat by dipping a wooden spoon into the hot oil; if it sizzles, it's ready. Add the potato wedges and fry until golden brown, about 10 minutes. BEAUTIFUL!

4 • Now back to the meat. To the skillet over medium heat, add the wedges of 1 tomato, 1 jalapeño, 1 serrano, and 1 cup of water; cover and cook until the meat is softened, about 10 minutes.

(recipe continues)

5 • Meanwhile, in a molcajete, grind the remaining shaved garlic clove into a paste with the remaining 1 tablespoon chicken bouillon powder. Grind in the remaining onion, then the other remaining ingredients, one at a time: the jalapeño, the serrano, and the remaining 2 tomatoes. Stir the mixture into the meat. Add the fried potato wedges and the cilantro. Stir until well combined, cover and simmer until all is tender, 8 to 10 minutes.

6 • Serve with rice and Refried Beans.

**Y LISTO AND ENJOY!**

# ENCHILADAS DE CARNE MOLIDA

## EN CHILE ROJO

Prep time: 15 minutes
Cook time: 20 minutes

SERVES 6 TO 8

Enchiladas are famous everywhere. They're known for being stuffed with cheese, but you can get really creative. My mother would stuff them with queso fresco, but we experimented as we got older. Shredded meat or any meat of choice works, but the ones with ground beef are what my kids really enjoyed growing up. Literally, enchiladas are one of the first ways a Mexican child is introduced to Mexican spices. They are palate trainers.

### For the Carne Molida (Ground Beef)

- 2 pounds (80/20) ground beef
- 1 white onion, diced
- 4 garlic cloves, minced
- 2 tablespoons Mesa Mia: Jenny's Favorite Seasoning

### For the Enchilada Sauce

- 6 dried guajillo chiles, seeded
- 2 dried puya chiles, seeded
- ½ white onion, roughly chopped
- 6 garlic cloves
- 2 tablespoons white vinegar
- 2 tablespoons chicken bouillon powder
- 1 teaspoon dried oregano
- 2 tablespoons pork lard (manteca)
- 2 tablespoons cornstarch
- ½ cup canola oil, divided
- 16 (6-inch) corn tortillas

### Toppings (optional)

Shredded lettuce

Dad's Tomatillo Salsa (page 179)

Sour cream

Crumbled queso fresco

1 • In a large skillet over medium-high heat, cook the ground beef, stirring frequently and breaking it up with a spoon, until browned, about 10 minutes. Drain off any excess oil that may have been released by the meat. Add the diced white onion, garlic, and seasoning; stir until well combined. Reduce the heat to medium-low and continue cooking, stirring frequently, until the onion is transparent, about 10 minutes.

2 • Meanwhile, make the Enchilada Sauce: In a medium saucepan, bring 1 cup of water to a boil, add the guajillos and pujas and boil until soft, about 15 minutes. Transfer the chiles and water to a blender, and add the onion, garlic, vinegar, chicken bouillon powder, and oregano; blend until no lumps are visible.

(recipe continues)

3 • In a separate medium saucepan over medium-low heat, melt the lard. Add the cornstarch, stirring constantly to dissolve and make a roux. Pour in the blended sauce, mix and bring it to a simmer; simmer until you've achieved the desired thickness, 5 to 7 minutes. I don't like it too thick, but the flavors need to come together. You can adjust the sauce depending on your preference; if you like it more on the thinner side, add a few tablespoons of water. Set aside.

4 • Now let's start making the enchiladas! Heat 2 tablespoons of canola oil in a small frying pan over medium-low heat. Grab one tortilla at a time with tongs, dip the entire tortilla in the sauce, until the tortilla is completely covered, drain off as much sauce as you can, and then fry the tortilla for 30 seconds on each side. The tortilla will get soft and begin to dissolve quickly so do this fast! Place on a plate and put 3 to 4 tablespoons of meat mixture down the center. Roll it up like a fat taquito, then transfer to a plate. Top it off with lettuce, salsa, sour cream, and queso fresco. Repeat with the remaining tortillas.

**Y LISTO AND ENJOY!**

# STEWS & SOUPS

## Birria de Res
(MEXICAN BEEF STEW)

## Carne en Su Jugo
(BEEF COOKED IN ITS OWN JUICES)

## Caldo de Albóndigas
(MEXICAN MEATBALL SOUP)

## Pozole Verde
(GREEN PORK AND CHICKEN STEW)

## Caldo de Res
(BEEF AND VEGETABLE SOUP)

# BiRRiA DE RES

Prep time: 15 minutes
Cook time: 2 hours 30 minutes
**SERVES 8 TO 10**

Aside from it being the recipe that kicked off my TikTok journey, this recipe is very special to me. It's my mom's, and every time there was a quinceanera or wedding or baptism, she would make this birria. The quinceanera represents the transition you make into womanhood at fifteen years old, leaving childhood behind. Padrinos come together and donate music or food to the party. Birria is kind of like a mole, in that it's made in huge pots which enables you to feed lots of people. My mom was known for making a really good one, and she continued to make it after moving to the United States. She became so known for it that people would pay her to make it, or she would donate the dish to the celebration.

All of my sisters (and I have five sisters, one brother!) ask my mom to make her birria, but she's eighty and I finally said it's time for us to learn. Covid forced me to . . . and I nailed it. It can be a little overwhelming looking down the long list of spices, but keep doing it and prac-tice will make you better. A lot of people ask if it's spicy. It's not, its more ancho chile flavored, which actually smells like a dried prune, more on the sweeter side. Birria is the complexity of Mexico in one dish. Each chile adds its own unique flavor.

I stick to my mom's recipe as much as I can, but sometimes you can't stop a whole recipe just because you're missing one ingredient. If you can't find certain types of chiles, you can substitute if you must. You can use California or New Mexico chiles in place of the gua-jillo chiles, for example. I have had to do this on occasion, and I figured if my mom couldn't really tell the difference, I am good. On Guy Fieri's show I was missing a lot of ingredients because they give you a budget and I couldn't afford all the spices. So, I had to focus on what was most important, and I was still able to pull it off, give them something good—and win.

(recipe continues on page 133)

8 pounds bone-in chuck beef roast

1¼ yellow onions, divided

1 whole garlic head plus 6 garlic cloves, divided

6 dried bay leaves, divided

3 tablespoons salt

5 dried California chiles, seeded and deveined

5 dried puya chiles, seeded and deveined

5 dried guajillo chiles, seeded and deveined

5 dried chiles de árbol, seeded and deveined

2 dried pasilla chiles, seeded and deveined

¼ cup white vinegar

2 tablespoons chicken bouillon powder

2 tablespoons toasted white sesame seeds

1 (1-inch) piece fresh ginger, peeled

2 tablespoons whole cumin seeds

2 tablespoons dried oregano

10 whole black peppercorns

4 whole cloves

## Toppings (optional)

1 medium yellow onion, diced

1 bunch fresh cilantro, roughly chopped

4 fresh limes, sliced into wedges

Chile de Aceite (page 174, optional)

## COOK'S NOTE

---

Traditionally birria is made with goat but you can substitute any meat. My mom also makes turkey, fish, and cactus (nopales) birria. Leftovers can be use to make Quesabirria Tacos (see page 57)!

1 • Place the beef in a large pot and add water until the water level is 4 inches above the meat. Add the whole onion, the whole garlic head, 4 bay leaves, and the salt. Cover the pot, bring the water to a boil, and boil for 1½ hours.

2 • Meanwhile, in a medium saucepan, add the California chiles, the puyas, guajillos, chiles de árbol, and pasillas and cover with water. Bring to a boil over medium-high heat and cook until the peppers are well rehydrated, about 10 minutes. Remove from the heat, allow to cool down, then drain the water.

3 • Once the meat has been cooking for 1½ hours, transfer the chiles to a blender along with 1 cup of the beef broth from the pot, the remaining ¼ onion, the 6 garlic cloves, the remaining 2 bay leaves, the vinegar, chicken bouillon powder, sesame seeds, ginger, cumin seeds, oregano, black peppercorns, and cloves. Blend until smooth. There should be no need to strain the mixture if you have a high-powered blender, but if the sesame seeds are still visible, then strain. Add the sauce to the pot with the meat, reduce the heat to a simmer, and continue cooking until the meat is tender, about 1 more hour.

4 • When the meat has cooked, take out a chunk and chop it up. Top it with onion and cilantro, a squeeze of lime, and a drizzle of Chile de Aceite, if desired.

**Y LISTO AND ENJOY!**

# CARNE EN SU JUGO

Prep time: 15 minutes
Cook time: 35 minutes
SERVES 6 TO 8

This is also a very popular beef stew, I think because of the green sauce. Before we started to see green pozole everywhere, this is the first thing we knew of, aside from traditional pork stew with green sauce that used green salsa. My mom wasn't familiar with this recipe as regional cooking styles are so different. This version came from my sister's mother-in-law who is from Guadalajara. We all fell in love.

You're cooking the beef in its own juices, so you don't really brown it to the point that you're frying it. It's nice and tender and the taste of the meat comes through and pairs well with the salsa. It was while making this dish that I first got the idea of using the broth I have on hand to make other salsas. Why not take advantage of all those deep, bone broth flavors? It really adds something different. But in this recipe, you stir the salsa into the beef and you serve it as a beef stew. I know it sounds like it is spicy, because of the jalapeños and serranos, but it's not. Little kids can eat this, and you can always add more chiles and hot sauce if you prefer. The toppings really make this stew different. You add bacon for crunch, more onion, radish, cilantro, avocado, queso fresco, and freshly cooked beans.

(recipe continues on page 136)

2 pounds beef shoulder (espadilla de res)

12 ounces bacon, diced

8 Mexican green onions, or 16 regular green onions

4 fresh guero chiles (yellow banana peppers)

12 green tomatillos

3 fresh jalapeños

4 fresh serrano chiles

1 white onion, roughly chopped

4 garlic cloves

3 tablespoons chicken bouillon powder

¼ teaspoon granulated sugar

## Toppings (optional)

Diced white onion

Diced radish

Chopped fresh cilantro

Diced avocado

Freshly cooked beans (see page 158)

Crumbled queso fresco

1 • Start by cutting the beef into small, ¼-inch pieces and set aside.

2 • Fry the bacon in a medium Dutch oven or pot over medium-high heat until crispy and the bacon fat is released, 8 to 10 minutes. Transfer the bacon to paper towels to soak up the excess oil. In the same pot with the bacon fat, over medium heat, cook the green onions and gueros, stirring constantly, until nicely browned, about 8 minutes. Remove from the pot and set aside. Once again in the same pot with the remaining bacon fat, over low heat, stir in the beef; cover the pot (very important to not fry the meat) and allow it to cook gently in its own juices until tender, about 15 minutes. Do not overcook, or the meat will become dry!

3 • While the meat is cooking, in a medium saucepan bring 4 cups of water to a boil over medium heat. Add the tomatillos, jalapeños, and serranos and cook until the tomatillos turn slightly brown, about 8 minutes. Immediately remove from the heat and put everything, including all the water, into a blender. Add the white onion, garlic, chicken bouillon powder, and sugar and blend until smooth.

4 • Once the meat is done cooking, pour the green sauce over the meat in the Dutch oven or pot. Add an extra cup of water to the blender, pulse to remove the green sauce stuck in the blender, and add that water to the pot as well. Increase the heat to medium-low, then stir in half of the bacon pieces (reserve the rest for topping), the green onions, and the gueros, and allow everything to simmer for the flavors to meld, about 15 minutes. BEAUTIFUL!!

5 • Now let's serve it up in a serving bowl! Top it off with the reserved bacon, onion, radish, cilantro, avocado, beans, and my special touch—queso fresco!

**Y LISTO AND ENJOY!**

# MEXICAN MEATBALL SOUP

# CALDO DE ALBÓNDIGAS

Prep time: 20 minutes
Cook time: 45 minutes

SERVES 8 TO 10

My dad was a really picky eater when my parents were married. When my mother would tell him she was going to make an albóndigas, he'd always respond with, "No let's go get food and bring it home." Finally, one day she just went ahead and made it—and he devoured it and wanted more. It was very different from his mother's, and now it's his favorite. Some people really don't add seasonings to their soup and it ends up not having enough "sazon," or flavor. You need to let it simmer, give it its time, and allow the flavors to come out. It's why things like soups and stews often taste better the next day. And Caldo de Albóndigas is another crowd favorite for cold weather.

2 pounds (80/20) ground beef

2 large eggs

1 white onion, diced, divided

½ cup basmati white rice

4 garlic cloves, minced

Leaves from 2 sprigs fresh mint, torn into little pieces

3 tablespoons ground New Mexico chile

2 tablespoons salt

1 tablespoon freshly ground black pepper

2 teaspoons dried oregano

2 tablespoons canola oil

1 Roma tomato, diced

2 tablespoons chicken bouillon powder

2 carrots, cut into 1-inch pieces

1 chayote squash, skin-on, cut into 1-inch cubes

4 Russet potatoes, skin-on, quartered

2 sprigs fresh sage

2 small Mexican squash (calabaza Mexicana), cut into 1-inch rounds (can also use zucchini)

## To Serve

Limes

Warm corn tortillas

Sour cream

Salsa de Tatemada Molcajete (page 177)

1 • In a large bowl, mix the beef and eggs. Then add half the diced onion, the rice, garlic, mint, New Mexico chile, salt, black pepper, and oregano, and mix everything well. Now you can start marking your meatballs; I like the size of my meatballs to be about 1½ inches in diameter. Just make sure you solidly pack the meatball so that it won't fall apart when it's boiling. When you are done forming them, you can put them back into the mixing bowl and set aside.

2 • Heat the oil in a large (8-quart) pot over medium heat, add the remaining onion, the diced tomato, and the chicken bouillon powder, and cook, stirring frequently, until the tomato is soft and the onion is translucent, about 5 minutes. Stir in the carrots,

(recipe continues on page 139)

chayote, and potatoes and cook until the flavors begin to meld, about 5 minutes. Add 5 quarts of water and the fresh sage. Increase the heat to medium-high and bring the broth to a boil. Reduce the heat to medium and add the meatballs; give it a quick stir, then add the Mexican squash (this way the squash is not too mushy). Cover the pot and cook until all the vegetables and the meatballs are tender and cooked through, about 15 minutes.

3 • Serve in bowls and top it off with your favorite toppings and a squeeze of lime juice. I enjoy my caldo with a corn tortilla with sour cream and Salsa Tatemada de Molcajete, rolled like a taquito on the side; you just dip it as you eat your soup. My kids still eat it like this!

**Y LISTO AND ENJOY.**

## GREEN PORK AND CHICKEN STEW

# POZOLE VERDE

Prep time: 20 minutes
Cook time: 1 hour 45 minutes
SERVES 8 TO 10

We didn't grow up eating Pozole Verde, but other parts of Mexico make it this way. It was eye-opening for us! It looks so pretty and sounds so fresh. Then, I found out you can make white pozole—without any sauce! Just spice it up with oregano, salt, onion, and bay leaves, so it's a colorless broth. But that doesn't sounds so appealing to me. These days, Pozole Verde is my immediate family's favorite. You use more fresh ingredients than you do for the basic pozole rojo, which uses the more economical dried chile pods. As a result, when we go to big gatherings we see more red pozole being served than verde.

2 pounds pork shoulder, cut in large (2- to 3-inch) cubes

1 whole garlic head, cut in half

1½ white onions, halved, divided

3 dried bay leaves

1 tablespoon salt

1 (110-ounce) can Mexican-style hominy

9 green tomatillos

1 bunch fresh cilantro

2 fresh jalapeño chiles

5 fresh serrano chiles

3 tablespoons chicken bouillon powder

1 tablespoon whole cumin seeds

3 sprigs fresh thyme

1 (4-pound) chicken, cut into 12 pieces

1 tablespoon dried oregano

### Toppings

1 white onion, diced

1 bunch fresh cilantro, chopped

½ head green cabbage, shredded

1 bunch radishes, thinly sliced into rounds

6 fresh limes, cut into wedges

Chile de Aceite (see page 174)

24 (6-inch) corn tostadas

1 • Fill a tall 10-quart pot with 6 quarts of water, and place over medium-high heat. Add the pork, garlic head, ½ onion, and bay leaves. Rinse the hominy in a colander to remove any residue, drain, and immediately add to pot along with the meat and salt; cover the pot and cook for 45 minutes.

2 • Meanwhile, to a blender, and 1 cup of the pork broth from the pot, the remaining ½ onion cut into quarters, the tomatillos, cilantro, jalapeños, serranos, chicken bouillon powder, cumin, and thyme. Blend until smooth.

3 • Once the pork has been cooking for 45 minutes, add the tomatillo mixture to the pot. Add the chicken and oregano and continue to cook until meat is tender, about 1 hour.

4 • Serve the pozole in a medium bowl and garnish it with your favorite toppings: onion, cilantro, green cabbage, radish, a squeeze of lime juice, and my favorite, Chile de Aceite! Enjoy with corn tostadas on the side.

# CALDO DE RES

Prep time: 15 minutes
Cook time: 2 hours 30 minutes
SERVES 8 TO 10

2 pounds of beef stew meat, cut into 1-inch chunks

2 pounds bone-in beef shank

1 white onion, halved

1 Roma tomato

1 garlic head

2 tablespoons salt

4 medium Russet potatoes, skin on and quartered

2 medium carrots, cut into 1-inch pieces

4 Mexican squash (calabaza Mexicana), cut into 1-inch pieces (can also use zucchini)

4 fresh ears corn, each cut into thirds

½ bunch fresh cilantro

1 green cabbage, quartered

## Toppings

Mexican Red Rice (page 146)

Lime wedges

Salsa Tatemada de Molcajete (page 177)

People from Michoacan, like my mother, uncles, and grandmother, would eat this with slices of banana, as well as rice, lime juice, and salsa. As we grew older, we just didn't do it anymore—but feel free to try it. You wouldn't think that it would go together and I thought it was so strange when I was little, but oddly enough it's really not bad! I think they would do this to fill us up, as beef was expensive.

It's perfect for a rainy day, and whenever it's cold, Caldo de Res sounds good to us. Honestly, though, it doesn't have to be cold . . . our moms would make this in 100°F weather. It's a bit of an inside joke. We'd be sweating and eating it—definitely a Mexican thing! When my mom would put the salsa de molcajete in the middle of the table I knew we were either having this or carne asada.

1 • Fill a tall, 10-quart pot with 5 quarts of water, and place over medium-high heat. Add the stew meat, beef shank, the onion, tomato, garlic, and salt; cover the pot and cook for 2 hours.

2 • After 2 hours, add the potatoes, carrots, Mexican quash, corn, and cilantro; cover the pot and cook for 30 minutes. Add the cabbage during the last 10 minutes of cooking and cook until tender. Remove the cabbage and cut each quarter in half; return it to the pot. Remove the beef shank, pull the meat off the bone, and cut the meat into 1-inch chunks; return the shank meat to the pot.

3 • Serve the Caldo de Res in bowls topped with Mexican Red Rice, lime juice, and Salsa Tatemada de Molcajete, my favorite!

Y LISTO AND ENJOY!

# RICE & BEANS

| | |
|---|---|
| **Arroz Rojo** (MEXICAN RED RICE) | **Frijoles Charros** (CHARRO BEANS) |
|  |  |
| **Cilantro Lime Rice** | **Frijoles Puercos** (PORK BEANS) |
|  |  |
| **Arroz Verde Poblano con Queso** (GREEN POBLANO CHEESE RICE) | **Frijoles Fritos** (REFRIED BEANS) |
| |  |

**Old-Fashioned Pinto Beans**

MEXICAN RED RICE

# ARROZ ROJO

**Prep time: 5 minutes**
**Cook time: 30 minutes**
**SERVES 6 TO 8**

As simple as this rice sounds, it has its own special technique and there can be pitfalls. If you don't follow the instructions to a "T," you can make it too mushy, or burn it, or leave it raw. It's very popular throughout Mexico. The way my mom makes it for me is probably the best one I've tried, and I've tried many out there. At some point here in the states, they started replacing the fresh tomatoes with paste and sauce, but it just doesn't have the same flavor. You have to fry the rice to a perfect golden brown. According to many grandmothers in Mexico, you cannot stop stirring or step away or you will burn it. The minute you step away, it's already burnt. The star of this rice is the fresh salsa, made with fresh garlic, tomatoes, and onion. It has to be the perfect measurements, and once it boils you have to reduce the heat so it will cook more slowly and create fluffy rice, that's not sticky or hard. One of the things my mom would insist on is that once you cover the rice, you DO NOT open the lid let. It cooks undisturbed for twenty-five minutes or you will get slapped on the hand! Otherwise, you release all the steam and the vapor. Never open the pot before its time. Sometimes with mole, too, the belief is that no one can come help you once you start making it, or you risk it becoming hard and cottage cheese–like, lumpy, or separating instead of smooth and silky. Might be a myth! But most of my aunts and uncles who cook believe this and will warn you away.

(recipe continues on page 148)

3 small Roma tomatoes

¼ small white onion, cut into ¼-inch wedges, divided

2 cloves garlic (1 whole, 1 minced), divided

4 tablespoons canola oil

2 cups basmati rice

2 tablespoons chicken bouillon powder

½ teaspoon fresh lime juice

**1** • To a blender, add the tomatoes, all the onion minus 2 wedges, the whole garlic clove, and 1 cup water; blend until smooth. Set aside.

**2** • In a medium saucepan, gently heat the oil over medium-low heat, but not too hot as the rice can burn fast. Add the rice and cook, stirring constantly, until lightly browned, about 3 minutes. Add the 2 reserved onion wedges and the minced garlic and continue to brown, stirring frequently, until the rice has achieved a deep golden-brown color, about 3 minutes.

**3** • Add the blended vegetables, 3 cups water, and the chicken bouillon powder and mix until well incorporated. Sprinkle the lime juice over top. Bring to a boil, then cover the saucepan, reduce the heat to low, and simmer until the rice has absorbed the liquid. Let rest for 5 minutes before opening the lid.

**Y LISTO AND ENJOY!**

# CILANTRO LIME RICE

Prep time: 10 minutes
Cook time: 30 minutes
**SERVES 6 TO 8**

3 tablespoons canola oil

2 cups basmati rice

¼ white onion, cut into ¼-inch wedges

1 garlic clove, crushed

2 tablespoons chicken bouillon powder

½ bunch fresh cilantro, roughly chopped

Juice of 2 fresh limes

This is one of our favorite warm-weather rices. It goes with almost any cuts of meat, but I catch myself serving it with fish, salmon, and shrimp. While we were stuck at the house during the pandemic we always hung out and cooked outside. Thankfully, we have a nice grill and pool and we didn't really feel like we were on lockdown. And thank god I like to buy in bulk! I always have so much food in my pantry. The lime is so fresh tasting, it's a summer or spring type of rice for me.

1 • Heat the oil in a medium saucepan over medium-low heat. Add rice and immediately stir, constantly, for 2 minutes. (Note: You do NOT brown the rice in this recipe.) Add the onion and garlic and cook, still stirring constantly, until the onion is translucent (but don't burn the garlic!), about 3 minutes. Increase the heat to medium, add 4 cups of water, give it a quick mix, then add the chicken bouillon powder; stir until well combined. When it begins to boil, reduce the heat to medium-low and cover the saucepan with a lid. Cook for 25 minutes. (Follow my mother's golden rule and do not uncover the pot until 25 minutes have passed.)

2 • Once you're ready to serve, uncover the pot, and stir in the cilantro, and squeeze lime juice all over. Stir and serve immediately.

**Y LISTO AND ENJOY!**

# ARROZ VERDE POBLANO

## CON QUESO

**Prep time: 10 minutes**
**Cook time: 30 minutes**
**SERVES 6 TO 8**

- 2 teaspoons plus 2 tablespoons canola oil, divided
- 4 fresh poblano peppers, julienned, divided
- ½ white onion, diced
- 2 garlic cloves, crushed
- 2 teaspoons chicken bouillon powder
- ½ bunch fresh cilantro
- 2 cups basmati rice
- 8 ounces Monterey Jack cheese, thinly sliced

It was—honestly—by accident that I came up with this recipe. I had extra poblanos and I had cheese. Usually, we used bell peppers, but since I had the poblanos I thought, why not? I have not gone back to bell peppers since. I love bell peppers, but this rice is so much better with the poblanos. Some people add corn, but I don't. My mother was always so surprised that my kids would get excited if they found the whole garlic cloves in the rice.

**1 •** In a medium skillet, heat 2 teaspoons of oil over medium heat. Add 2 of the poblanos and cook, stirring frequently, until they start to become tender, 4 to 5 minutes. Stir in the onion, garlic, and chicken bouillon powder, and cook, stirring constantly, until the onion begins to soften, about 2 minutes. Transfer half of the poblano mixture plus the cilantro and 1 cup of water to a blender and blend until smooth. Set aside.

**2 •** In the same saucepan over medium-low heat, heat the remaining 2 tablespoons oil. Add the rice and cook, stirring constantly, until the rice is lightly browned, about 5 minutes. Add the reserved poblano strip mixture and cook for 3 minutes, stirring. Add the blended green sauce and 3 cups water. Mix well. BEAUTIFUL! Cover the saucepan with a lid and cook for 25 minutes. Five minutes before the rice is done, lay slices of cheese over the rice. Cover the saucepan again with the lid and allow the cheese to melt. It's ready to serve.

**Y LISTO AND ENJOY!**

## CHARRO BEANS

# FRIJOLES CHARROS

Prep time: 10 minutes
Cook time: 2 hours
SERVES 8 TO 10

**Ingredients:**

1½ pounds dried pinto beans, rinsed

1 pound cueritos (pork skin)

1½ white onions, divided

2 garlic cloves

2 teaspoons salt

1 pound bacon, cut into ½-inch-long pieces

1 (16-ounce) package beef hotdogs, sliced into rounds

2 fresh jalapeño chiles, sliced into rounds

2 fresh guero chiles (yellow banana peppers), sliced into rounds

1 pound pork chorizo

1 beefsteak tomato, diced

1 bunch fresh cilantro

These beans make a great midnight snack, and they're always perfect as the sun goes down when we go camping. (Cowboy style, they'd be under the stars eating this, wherever they'd rested their horses!) The beans are packed with ingredients. Eat as a side or sort of like a soup! I cook them low and slow, because if you cook pinto beans on high they burst. Take your time over medium-low heat and they come out perfect. We like them more soupy than stewy, so I always make sure I've added plenty of water. It's all about preference.

1 • In a 10- to 12-quart pot, bring 8 quarts of water to a boil over high heat. Add the beans, cueritos, the whole onion cut in half, the garlic, and salt. Cover and cook for 1 hour.

2 • Heat a medium skillet over medium heat, and cook the bacon pieces, stirring frequently, until crispy, about 10 minutes. Transfer the bacon to paper towels to absorb the excess fat. In the same skillet with the bacon fat, over medium heat, cook the hot dogs, stirring frequently, until lightly browned, about 8 minutes. Dice the remaining ½ onion and add to the skillet; cook, stirring, until it releases its aromas, about 2 minutes. Add the jalapeños and gueros, and cook, stirring constantly, until the flavors are melded, 2 to 3 minutes. Remove all from the skillet and set aside.

3 • In the same skillet over medium heat, cook the chorizo, stirring constantly, until browned, about 8 minutes. Add the tomato and cook, stirring, until softened, about 5 more minutes.

4 • Once the beans have been cooking for an hour, add the bacon, hot dog mixture, chorizo mixture, and half of the cilantro to the beans. Give it a good mix and add more water, if needed. The beans should be soupy. Cover and gently simmer over medium-low heat for another hour to ensure the beans are tender.

PORK BEANS

# FRiJOLES PUERCOS

**Prep time: 5 minutes**
**Cook time: 20 minutes**
**SERVES 6 TO 8**

1½ cups pork lard

2 (16-ounce) tubes pork chorizo

1½ pounds cooked pinto beans (see page 158)

1 pound Chihuahua cheese, shredded, divided

1 (190-ml) bottle salsa Huichol®, Valentina, or Tapatio hot sauce

1 (7-ounce) can pickled jalapeños, julienned, pickle juice reserved

1 cup green olives, pitted

People often confuse this dish with frijoles charros, but it's another example of a Mexican recipe that has similar (in this case, less) ingredients but a different method—which changes everything. These beans are popular in Mexico because they are served at big events with barbacoa and birria, much like the Mexican wedding pasta. These were always the beans you'd find on the table. You have to mash them up at the end, sort of like refried beans but with all these flavors happening together. The pitted olives you leave until the end, to garnish. Huichol is a very popular salsa brand from Nayarit where my husband is from. The indigenous men have a special way of dressing, they decorate their hats, so that's image you find on the bottle.

1 • In a deep, large skillet melt the lard over medium-low heat. Add the chorizo and cook, stirring frequently, until dark brown, about 10 minutes. Add the beans (for this dish, the beans must be extra smooth) and simmer until all the flavors have melded, about 10 minutes. With an immersion blender, blend the beans and chorizo mixture until silky smooth.

2 • Set aside 1 cup cheese for topping. Stir in the remaining cheese, the salsa, and the reserved juice from the pickled jalapeños. Top the beans off sprinkled with the reserved 1 cup cheese, then add the pickled jalapeños and olives to form a crown around the pot, for presentation.

**Y LISTO AND ENJOY!**

# FRiJOLES FRiTOS

Prep time: 5 minutes
Cook time: 20 minutes
**SERVES 6 TO 8**

1 cup pork lard

2 dried chiles de árbol

8 cups freshly cooked Old-Fashioned Pinto Beans (page 158)

Everybody that comes to my house says my refried beans are perfect, and I gotta say it's due to the pork lard. You have to allow it to simmer so that the flavors marry. The lard must be hot, do not add beans to cold lard—it's the number one mistake people make. Just be careful not to get burned, lard can quickly go up in flames!

1 • In a large, deep pot, over medium heat, melt the lard and increase the heat to medium-high. Turn off the heat. Quickly add the chiles de árbol and cook until just darkened and lightly fried, 20 to 30 seconds, then remove and set aside. Next, start adding the beans in 2-cup batches, it's very important that the lard is hot, but be careful not to get burned as lard can splatter. Use the lid to help protect you from splatter by covering the pot partially with the lid, then adding the batches of beans, and covering the pot completely in between batches.

2 • When all the beans have been added, cover the pot and turn the heat to medium; allow the beans to simmer and absorb the pork lard flavor, 10 to 15 minutes. Mash by hand with a masher or with an immersion blender until smooth. Top with the fried chiles de árbol.

**Y LISTO AND ENJOY!**

# OLD-FASHIONED PINTO BEANS

**Prep time: 5 minutes**
**Cook time: 2 hours 30 minutes**
**MAKES 9 CUPS, SERVES 10 TO 12**

3 cups dried pinto beans, rinsed

1½ tablespoons salt

Fill a pot with 12 cups of water, add the beans and salt, cover, and bring to a boil over medium-high heat. Reduce the heat to medium-low and cook the beans until tender, aboaut 2 hours. Drain.

**Y LISTO AND ENJOY!**

My mother always had freshly cooked beans on the stove, so it was always part of the aromas of my house. Pinto beans are something that we keep on hand as it's an easy side dish and a staple of Mexican cuisine. I am used to making huge pots of beans and freezing them, but it's better to have fresh, of course. My mother-in-law would never freeze beans, but when you're a working mom, you must help yourself out in some ways. One of the secrets to cooking pinto beans is to add enough water to ensure that they stay beautifully pink and do not become dark. You're cooking them for a few hours after all! This is the most traditional, old-fashioned way to make them. You can add onion, cilantro, and garlic, but if you're going to refry them in lard anyway then you don't have to worry about having enough flavor. What you need is the base flavor of pinto beans and salt.

# TORTILLAS, SALSAS & MORE

**Homemade Flour Tortillas**

**Homemade Corn Tortillas**

**Chorizo Flour Tortillas**

**Salsa con Queso**
(SALSA WITH CHEESY CHUNKS)

**Salsa Taquera**
(TACO STAND SALSA)

**Salsa Cruda**
(RAW SALSA)

**Chile de Aceite**
(CHILI OIL)

**Salsa Tatemada de Molcajete**

**Ahumada Salsa Morita**
(SMOKY MORITA SALSA)

**Dad's Tomatillo Salsa**

**Mom's Tomato Sauce**

# HOMEMADE FLOUR TORTILLAS

Prep time: 10 minutes
Cook time: 20 minutes

**MAKES ABOUT 15 TORTILLAS**

3 cups all-purpose flour, plus more for dusting

½ cup pork lard

1 cup warm water

2 teaspoons salt

When we got to the United States, my mother was always working and more worried about making ends meet, than making things from scratch (we are a family of eight after all), so I didn't learn from her how to make flour tortillas. But when we went back to Mexico, just across the border, my cousin Erika was working in a little factory that made tortillas. She became good at it and she started making them at home. I was so surprised at what a huge difference it creates to make them from scratch. It melts in your mouth, and you don't even feel full. They're dangerous! It comes down to using fresh ingredients and no preservatives. She makes them so thin that you could eat twenty of them. I asked her to teach me, but I am not a baker and I struggled to get it. My daughter is a great baker and she picked it up right away and started making them at home. I put on my big girl pants and, sure enough, eventually I got it right, but my daughter is still better than me. When we visit Mexico, Erika has dozens of these ready for us to eat. She likes to put butter on fresh warm tortillas and gives it to the kids, kind of like bread, with juice or coffee. These flavors are not found in a store-bought package.

1 • Start by creating a mountain out of the flour on a clean countertop. Create a well in the center of the flour. Add the lard to the well and pour the warm water over the lard. The warm water will dissolve the lard. Add the salt. With your fingers, slowly bring the flour into the well and mix it into the liquid, until all the water and lard are absorbed by the flour. Once you have formed a dough ball, knead it with your hands until the dough is nice and smooth, about 5 minutes. Cover with plastic wrap and set aside.

2 • Clean the surface well, making sure there are no crumbs. Roll the dough out to 12 inches long (loaf-like style). With your hand (thumb and index finger) pinch off a dough ball that is 2 inches in diameter. Roll the dough ball with your palm in a circular motion on a flat surface to help create a nice round shape. Dust extra flour on the countertop and press the dough ball with two fingers to flatten the dough, at the same time dusting with flour to prevent it from sticking on the countertop when rolling out. Before rolling out, press all around the edges with your finger to help roll out more easily. With a lightly floured rolling pin, start rolling and stretching the dough out to 3 inches, then flip, roll again, and repeat the stretching 3 to 4 times until you have stretched it out to a 10-inch diameter (they don't have to be perfectly round if you are a first timer).

3 • Heat a large comal or skillet over medium-low heat. Place the tortilla on the comal until you see bubbles forming, about 1 minute, then flip and heat for another minute. Wrap in a clean kitchen towel to keep soft. Repeat the process with the rest of the dough. Note that these tortillas are not fully cooked, they are made to be heated again when ready to be served. Once cooled, store in the fridge in a resealable bag for up to 2 weeks.

# HOMEMADE CORN TORTILLAS

Prep time: 1 hour 20 minutes
Cook time: 20 minutes
**MAKES 18 TO 24 TORTILLAS**

Here's another item where the homemade version is just so much better than the store bought! You can easily eat a dozen. I recommend the Maseca brand's yellow corn flour, called Amarillo, for making these tortillas. And I learned this trick from my followers: to get the best results, use a thin plastic produce bag from the produce aisle to sandwich the dough in the press and prevent it from sticking. I used to use a resealable plastic bag, but according to my followers that is too thick. The produce bag makes it easy.

## COOK'S NOTE

My mom and I keep a cup of water to dab our fingers and keep them moist as we go. The little bit of water helps to hydrate the masa and it makes it easier to press the dough. The key is to not have cracks or else it won't inflate or puff up.

4 cups corn flour
(I recommend Maseca
Amarillo brand)

3 cups warm water

1 teaspoon salt

**Equipment**

Tortilla press

1 • In a large bowl, combine the corn flour, water, and salt and mix well; knead for 10 minutes. The dough will be ready when the masa doesn't stick to your hands. Set the dough aside to rest for 1 hour.

2 • Heat a nonstick comal or skillet over medium-high heat. With clean hands, grab a 2-inch dough ball, knead it for another 20 to 30 seconds with your hands, then place it on the tortilla press (see Cook's Note). Using a thin grocery produce bag, sandwich the dough between the plastic so it doesn't stick to the press and the tortilla comes out nice and thin. Gently press until the dough is completely flattened out into a 6-inch round. Peel off the plastic from both sides to remove the tortilla.

3 • Place the tortilla on the comal or skillet and count for 10 to 12 seconds or (as my mom says) watch for when the tortilla starts to dance (it slides side to side), then give it a first flip and cook for 60 seconds. Once you see the soft masa starting to cook on the edges, give it its final flip and gently tap the center of the tortilla. That's when you will see the magic of the heat, as it makes the tortilla rise and inflate. Let it cook for another 30 to 40 seconds and BEAUTIFUL! It's ready. As you make the tortillas, immediately wrap them in a kitchen towel (tortillero) so that they won't dry out. Continue making the remaining tortillas. It's very important not to flip more than two times, and to cover once cooked to prevent them from getting hard and crusty.

**Y LISTO AND ENJOY!**

# CHORIZO FLOUR TORTILLAS

Prep time: 10 minutes
Cook time: 20 minutes
**MAKES ABOUT 20 TORTILLAS**

Everybody loves chorizo ... and my homemade flour tortillas. When my followers see my cousin Erika making these, it goes viral. She's so good at it, her technique is incredibly fast. I came up with this idea after watching people make beet- or spinach-flavored tortillas. I thought, I can do this with chorizo! Adding chorizo means the dough is not as smooth, but it inflates as it cooks, and it has so much flavor.

4 tablespoons cooked
   pork chorizo

4 tablespoons chorizo oil
   (reserved after cooking
   the chorizo)

4 cups all-purpose flour,
   plus more for dusting

½ cup pork lard

1¼ cups hot water

2 teaspoons baking
   powder

1 • Start by combining the chorizo with the oil in a blender until smooth. On a flat, clean surface, make a mountain with the flour, then create a well in the center. Add the blended chorizo meat and oil to the well, then add the lard and hot water. The warm water will melt the lard. Sprinkle in the baking powder. With a wooden spoon, bring the flour into the crater to combine with the hot water. When your hands can handle the heat of the water, start kneading the dough. It will feel sticky, but keep on kneading and trust the process. Knead until the dough is soft and smooth, 5 to 7 minutes. Cover the dough with plastic wrap and set aside.

2 • Clean the surface well, making sure there are no crumbs left behind. Roll the dough out to 12 inches long (loaf-like style).

3 • With your hand (thumb and index finger) pinch off a dough ball that is 2 inches in diameter. Roll the dough ball with your palm in a circular motion on a flat surface to help create a nice round shape. Dust extra flour on the countertop and press the dough ball with two fingers to flatten the dough, at the same time dusting with flour to prevent it from sticking to the countertop when rolling it out. Before rolling it, press all around the edges with your finger to help roll it out more easily. Lightly dust a rolling pin with flour, and start rolling and stretching the dough out to 3 inches, then flip, roll again, and repeat the stretching 3 to 4 times until you have stretched it out to an 8-inch diameter (they don't have to be perfectly round if you are a first timer). BEAUTIFUL!

4 • Place the tortilla on the comal or skillet and heat through until you see bubbles, about 1 minute. Flip and heat for another minute, then wrap in a clean kitchen towel to keep soft. Repeat the process with the remaining dough. Note that these tortillas are not fully cooked, they are made to be heated again when ready to be served. Once they are cooled, store in the fridge in a resealable bag for up to 2 weeks.

## SALSA WITH CHEESY CHUNKS

# SALSA CON QUESO

**Prep time: 5 minutes**
**Cook time: 18 minutes**
**SERVES 4 TO 6**

1 tablespoon canola oil

1 white onion, diced

3 fresh serrano chiles, diced

4 Roma tomatoes, diced

1 teaspoon salt

16 ounces queso panela, cut into ½-inch cubes

For Serving

Refried Beans (page 157)

Homemade Flour Tortillas (page 162)

When I am looking for a quick or easy breakfast, or I don't have meat ready to go, I make homemade tortillas and this salsa and have myself an easy-to-make breakfast. Other times I will make this salsa and serve it with quesadillas. The secret is allowing the tomato, onion, and cheese to infuse together. The method creates a unique flavor. This is another recipe we like to take when we go camping. I can do anything I want from scratch in my cast-iron skillets. I take my whole cooler full of fresh ingredients, no cans, and whole eggs. My husband is so good at organizing and stacking it all, he makes it so easy for me. I don't even miss my fridge. I hate it if I forget an ingredient, but we just make it happen. And we do it every year, sometimes twice a year. Now we're able to rent RVs and some people say we're glamping, but I am still cooking outside! It sucks to cook in an RV, there's no space!

Heat the oil in a large, deep skillet over medium-high heat. Add the onion and serranos and cook, stirring occasionally, until the onion is translucent, about 3 minutes. Add the tomatoes and salt and cook, stirring constantly, until the tomatoes begin to soften, about 5 minutes. Then add the queso panela and simmer, stirring frequently, until the salsa has reduced and the flavors have melded, about 10 minutes. The cheese won't melt, it will stay as cubes sort of like firm tofu. And as easy as that, you have prepared this authentic, flavorful dish. Now you can enjoy it as a side with my refried beans and tortillas. Refried Beans and Homemade Flour Tortillas.

**Y LISTO AND ENJOY!**

## TACO STAND SALSA

# SALSA TAQUERA

Prep time: 5 minutes
Cook time: 10 minutes
**MAKES ABOUT 2 CUPS,
SERVES 4 TO 6**

½ white onion, halved

3 Roma tomatoes

14 dried chiles de árbol, stemmed

2 tablespoons canola oil

3 garlic cloves

1½ tablespoons chicken bouillon powder

We call this Salsa Taquera because it goes with pretty much any taco, and 98 percent of the taquerias (taco stands) in Mexico have this salsa on hand. Fourteen chiles de árbol sounds like a lot, and perhaps it could be spicy for someone if they have never tasted chiles, so you can adjust the amount if you like. But this is the way I make it; and the way I see things, if you make a salsa that is not spicy it's gone in no time, but if you make it spicy people need to use only a little bit and you will have salsa left over! It isn't satisfying if it isn't spicy. I am like my dad, we can have three salsas in front of us and we'll look for the spiciest. At restaurants we ask for four hot sauces and test them all out. We try both red and green salsas—always on the hunt for the spicy one.

1 • Heat a large, dry comal or large skillet over medium-high heat. Roast the onion, tomatoes, and chiles de árbol, turning frequently, for 5 minutes until they are nicely charred. (Be careful! Charring chiles de árbol can make the whole house cough, the spice vapors are real!)

2 • In a large skillet, heat the oil over medium heat. Add the roaasted onion and cook, stirring constantly, until it begins to soften, separating the onion pieces with your spoon, about 3 minutes. Add the roasted tomatoes and chiles de árbol and the garlic and cook until the garlic flavor is infused into the oil, about 3 minutes. Be careful not to burn the garlic. Transfer everything to a blender, including the oil from the pan. Add the chicken bouillon powder and ½ cup water and blend until smooth. Serve in a small bowl.

**Y LISTO AND ENJOY!**

# SALSA CRUDA

Prep time: 5 minutes
Cook time: 5 minutes
**MAKES ABOUT 2 CUPS, SERVES 4 TO 6**

4 Roma tomatoes, roughly chopped

4 fresh serrano chiles, roughly chopped

4 dried chiles de árbol, stemmed and roughly chopped

½ white onion, roughly chopped

3 garlic cloves

1 tablespoon chicken bouillon powder

Add the tomatoes, serranos, chiles de árbol, onion, garlic, and chicken bouillon powder to a blender and pulse. As you combine the mixture, make sure to pulse on and off; you don't want the salsa to turn into a smoothie, you want everything to blend but remain a bit chunky. BEAUTIFUL! As easy as that, it's ready. Transfer to a serving bowl.

**Y LISTO AND ENJOY!**

Salsa Cruda is kind of like a pico de gallo but turned into a salsa. The difference is, we are not adding cilantro, and it's spicier. In addition to the serranos, there's a bit of heat from the chiles de árbol. And I can't leave out the chicken bouillon powder, it's my salt replacement and it's a staple in a Mexi can house. This specific salsa was created by my cousin's uncle, not by someone on my side of the family. My cousin does not want to share the actual secret ingredients, so I did my best to re-create the flavors. Her uncle created his wealth by selling fried chicken necks! I am a big turkey neck lover, and I am always hunting for it. But imagine, he built a business on something that people would often throw away. He fries them up and people eat them like appetizers, on a paper nacho plate with ten little necks and Salsa Cruda on the side. Amazing how well he's done—he draws a big crowd!

CHILI OIL

# CHiLE DE ACEiTE

Prep time: 5 minutes
Cook time: 8 minutes
MAKES ABOUT 1½ CUPS

1 cup olive oil

100 chiles de árbol, stemmed

2 garlic cloves

1 tablespoon chicken bouillon powder

1 • Heat the olive oil in a large, deep skillet over medium-low heat. Add the chiles to the skillet in batches and lightly fry them, stirring constantly, then remove them as soon as they turn bright red in color, about 5 minutes per batch. Make sure you don't burn them. Transfer them to a plate to cool. Remember to open all the windows and doors, if possible, or else the entire house will start coughing! Reserve the oil and set it aside to cool.

2 • Transfer the chiles de árbol to a blender with the garlic and chicken bouillon powder. Drizzle the reserved oil into the blender slowly as you blend. I like it to be paste-like, instead of chunks. Now it's ready, BEAUTIFUL! Serve in a small bowl.

Y LISTO AND ENJOY!

This is my famous chile oil, and the subject of one of my viral videos. A lot of people would say this is macha chile, but macha has peanuts and this one here is just the chile de árbol. And I like to flavor it with garlic and chicken bouillon powder, the original recipe just has the chiles. I have to have this on my table. When it's gone, my friends and family revolt. Just add a couple drops to your soup or use the paste that settles at the bottom in your pozole or menudo. It's really similar to straight hot sauce. Be careful because the heat will depend on the harvest; the peppers are not as spicy in some seasons as others. Warning: If you over-fry the chiles, it is like tear gas—you cannot breathe. There's an inside joke, if you grew up in a Mexican household you would often have to run outside when the house became filled with chile smoke! It's bad news if you're not careful—do not burn the chiles and do not let the olive oil boil or get too hot. This goes well with menudo and pozoles (see pages 141).

## COOK'S NOTE

This chili oil can last for a month unrefrigerated, because it is covered in oil. Refrigerated, it can last for 3 months. You'll eat it slowly, in small amounts, because it's so spicy.

# SALSA TATEMADA DE MOLCAJETE

Prep time: 5 minutes
Cook time: 10 minutes
MAKES ABOUT 1½ CUPS

4 Roma tomatoes

4 fresh serrano chiles

3 garlic cloves

1 tablespoon chicken bouillon powder

¼ white onion, diced

4 sprigs fresh cilantro, roughly chopped

The molcajete comes out for this recipe, and when it does, we know we're having carne asada or Caldo de Res. If you don't have a molcajete, get one. I cannot completely explain the difference in flavor between making this in a blender versus a molcajete, but when we have time, as when cooking outside or camping, we find that difference is profound. It is not the same. Perhaps the sharp blades of the blender affect the flavor because in a molcajete you're grinding the ingredients against a rock and you seem to experience the release of more of the natural oils. I prefer not to grind the diced onion and cilantro and mix them in at the end.

My mother-in-law's Salsa Taremada de Molcajete is a bit different, she loves chiles de árbol, and first toasts them on the comal, then grinds them, then grinds in the garlic and salt, and finally grinds in the roasted Roma tomatoes—but she uses no onion or cilantro. It's really good, too, and that version goes well with chicharrones, fried pork skins. Everyone has their own style of molcajete.

1 • In a dry, medium cast-iron skillet over medium high heat, roast the Roma tomatoes, turning them as needed, until charred, about 3 minutes. Add the serranos and garlic to the skillet and roast until charred, occasionally turning them, about 5 minutes. Remove from the heat.

2 • In a medium molcajete, combine the garlic and chicken bouillon powder and grind them into a paste. Add the serranos and grind them into the mixture. Then add the Roma tomatoes and mash them into the mixture—you don't want to grind them too much; you want to keep the tomatoes chunky. Stir in the diced onion and chopped cilantro with a spoon. Do not mash or grind them. BEAUTIFUL! The great thing about using the molcajete is that is acts as a serving bowl.

**Y LISTO AND ENJOY!**

# AHUMADA
# SALSA MORITA

**Prep time: 5 minutes**
**Cook time: 10 minutes**
**MAKES 1 ½ TO 2 CUPS**

4 Roma tomatoes

6 fresh red jalapeño chiles (adjust amount to your heat level)

4 dried morita chiles

¼ white onion

3 garlic cloves

2 tablespoons chicken bouillon powder

In a saucepan, bring 1 cup water to a boil over medium-high heat. Add the tomatoes, jalapeños, and moritas and boil until softened, about 10 minutes. Transfer the vegetables and their liquid to a blender, and add the onion, garlic, and chicken bouillon powder. Blend until smooth and serve!

**Y LISTO AND ENJOY!**

I was not familiar with morita chiles, and I fell in love with them when I learned how to make this salsa. It's a red jalapeño that is dried and smoked, with a dark berry, smoky flavor, similar in some ways to a chipotle but dried and spicier. Moritas come from Puebla, and you can find them in Veracruz cooking as well. Combine them with tomatillos or use them alone. They're perfect with eggs, tortilla chips as a dip, or even with chicken. The salsa turns a deep brick red color. I like an extra kick so I add fresh red jalapeños—morita chiles along aren't spicy enough for us! Remember, any salsa made at home is better than any bought in a store.

# DAD'S TOMATILLO SALSA

Prep time: 5 minutes
Cook time: 8 minutes

MAKES 2½ CUPS

1 pound milpero
   tomatillos
12 to 15 dried chiles de
   árbol, stemmed
½ white onion
2 tablespoons chicken
   bouillon powder
¼ teaspoon sugar

Bring a medium pot filled with water to a boil over medium-high heat. Add the tomatillos and chile de árbol and boil until the tomatillos are beginning to brown and just barely softened (try to not allow them to burst), about 8 minutes. Drain the tomatillos and peppers and transfer to a blender. Add the onion, chicken bouillon powder and (my dad's recipe secret SHHH!) the sugar, and blend until smooth. BEAUTIFUL! Pour the green salsa into a serving bowl.

**Y LISTO AND ENJOY!**

I call this my dad's tomatillo salsa because as we were growing up my dad would always guide my sister Tita as she made it. I remember him telling her to add this and that. His secret is to add sugar to this salsa, and I've never seen anyone else do that—I was so surprised. But it balances out the bitterness of the tomatillos. People think it will turn out to be sweet, but it's such a small amount you can't taste the sugar. The bigger the tomatillo the more bitter it is, and milpero tomatillos are very small. They're so small that they're rarely, if ever, sold in bulk bins. Look for them prepackaged by the pound in a mesh bag.

# MOM'S TOMATO SAUCE

Prep time: 5 minutes
Cook time: 8 minutes
MAKES ABOUT 2 CUPS

4 Roma tomatoes

3 fresh jalapeños

1½ tablespoons chicken bouillon powder

¼ white onion, diced

½ fresh orange

½ fresh lime

1 teaspoon dried oregano leaves

This is my mom's version of the canned brand El Pato Salsa de Jalapeño. We fell in love with this because our tradition is to use this sauce whenever we make fried tacos or tamales. Even though it has three jalapeños, it's not spicy. Some people, also from Michoacan, use the pickled jalapeños and the pickle juice from the can and you can add them to make it spicier, but I prefer using only the fresh jalapeños.

Bring a medium pot with 2 cups of water to a boil over medium-high heat. Add the tomatoes and jalapeños and boil until tomatoes are very soft, about 10 minutes. Transfer the tomatoes, jalapeños, 1 cup of the cooking water, and the chicken bouillon powder to a blender and blend until smooth. BEAUTIFUL! Now transfer to a serving bowl and stir in the onion. Squeeze in the orange and lime juice, sprinkle in the oregano, and give it a quick mix. I like to take the dried oregano leaves and rub them it between the palms of my hands to grind them a little finer before adding them.

**Y LISTO AND ENJOY!**

# DESSERTS

**Mexican Churros**

**Pastel De Zanahoria**
(CARROT WALNUT CAKE)

**Paletas de Pepino, Pina, y Menta**
(MINT, PINEAPPLE, AND CUCUMBER POPSICLES)

**Rompope Bolis**
(EGG NOG POPSICLES)

**Flan de Leche**
(CARAMELIZED CUSTARD)

**Garapiñado**
(CARAMELIZED PECANS)

**Postre de Calabaza**
(CANDIED PUMPKIN)

**Capirotada Estilo Michoacan**
(MEXICAN BREAD PUDDING)

**Conchas**
(SWEET BREAD)

**Rosca de Reyes**
(THREE KINGS BREAD)

**Buñuelos**
(MEXICAN SWEET FRITTERS)

**Polvorones**
(SNOWBALLS)

# MEXICAN CHURROS

Prep Time: 15 minutes
Cook Time: 30 minutes
SERVES 4 TO 6

1 stick (8 tablespoons) unsalted butter

½ cup plus 2 tablespoons granulated sugar, divided

Pinch of salt

2 cups all-purpose flour

3 large eggs

2 tablespoons ground cinnamon

2 cups canola oil

To Serve

Cajeta (milk caramel sauce)

Chocolate dip

When I was a little girl, my dad worked in a donut factory and would come home smelling like donuts and sugar—I used to love to smell his hands! He'd bring home extra donuts, too, and tell us, if you want to make extra money, you can sell them to the neighbors. So, I'd go knocking on doors to earn my spending money. When dad left the donut factory to work in a Lovely Pies factory (they're like fruit-filled hand pies) I had to come up with something else, and my creative sales side came out. I'd buy 5 churros for a dollar from an old man who sold them from a basket on the back of his bicycle. Then I'd knock on doors selling them two for a dollar—and the neighbors would buy them!

Churros are the most famous dessert from Mexico these days, and you can find churros-flavored everything, from cheesecake to ice cream. There's some technique involved, such as ensuring there are no air pockets in the dough, but they're so easy to make once you get the hang of it.

1 • Fill a small saucepan over medium-high heat with 1 cup of water, the butter, 2 tablespoons of sugar, and the salt. Bring it to a boil and allow the butter to melt. Reduce the heat to low and add the flour a bit at a time, stirring constantly until completely combined; set aside to cool.

2 • Transfer the batter to a bowl and stir in the eggs, one at a time, mixing thoroughly each time. Mix well to release any air pockets, so that it becomes nice and smooth. Transfer the mixture to a piping bag with a 2-inch star tip. In a shallow bowl, mix the remaining ½ cup sugar with the cinnamon until well combined. Set aside.

3 • Heat the oil in a large skillet over medium heat. Check the heat by dipping a wooden spoon into the hot oil; if it sizzles, it's ready. Pipe the churro out into the hot oil and cut the dough to your desired length with scissors as it comes out. You can make them bite-size or, like I do, about 5 to 6 inches long. Fry in batches until golden brown and cooked through, 4 to 5 minutes on each side; do not overcrowd. Drain on paper towels and toss in the cinnamon sugar. Serve with Cajeta or a chocolate dip.

Y LISTO AND ENJOY!

# PASTEL DE ZANAHORIA

Prep time: 30 minutes
Cook time: 1 hour

**SERVES 6 TO 8**

None of my family members like having cake for our birthdays, we're more into pastries, and would rather have a little mountain of donuts than a cake. But when we do have cake, we ask my daughter to make this one. A delicious carrot cake trumps chocolate cake every time for us, even when bought from the pastry shop. I used to give out little pieces of cake at family gatherings, not understanding that people really wanted humungous slices. I just don't get it!

## For the Cake

2½ cups plus ¾ cup all-purpose flour, divided

2 teaspoons baking soda

2 teaspoons baking powder

1 teaspoon ground cinnamon

½ teaspoon ground cardamon

½ teaspoon ground allspice

¼ teaspoon ground ginger

1½ teaspoons salt

1⅔ cups granulated sugar

1 cup light brown sugar

¾ cup sour cream

¾ cup vegetable oil

½ cup applesauce

3 large eggs

2 teaspoons pure vanilla extract

1 cup chopped walnuts (or pecans), toasted

1 pound carrots, finely shredded

## For the Frosting

2 cups (4 sticks) unsalted butter, at room temperature

16 ounces cream cheese, at room temperature

12 ounces butter, room temp

7 cups (1¾ pounds) confectioners' sugar

1 teaspoon pure vanilla extract

1 • Preheat the oven to 350°F. Line the bottom of three 8-inch cake pans with parchment paper. I like to cut the paper to the shape of the pans; this makes it easy to remove the cake. To hold the paper in place, rub a bit of butter on the bottom and sides of the pan and then dust the sides with 1 tablespoon of flour.

2 • MAKE THE CAKE: Sift the dry ingredients into a large mixing bowl: 2½ cups of flour, the baking soda, baking powder, cinnamon, cardamom, allspice, ginger, and salt. Whisk it all together. In a medium bowl mix together the granulated sugar, light brown sugar, sour cream, oil, applesauce, eggs, and vanilla. Place the walnuts in a small bowl and toss with the remaining ¾ cup flour. Pour the wet ingredients into the dry ingredients and mix. Add the walnuts and carrots and continue mixing until well combined. Divide the batter equally between the 3 cake pans. Bake for 40 to 45 minutes, or until a toothpick inserted in the center comes out clean. Set aside to cool completely before removing the cakes from the pans.

3 • MAKE THE FROSTING: In a large mixing bowl, cream the butter and cream cheese using a hand mixer. Add the confectioners' sugar and vanilla and mix until combined (but be careful because you may make a mess!). Make sure your cake is completely cooled down or the frosting will melt. Starting with one cake as the base, generously top it with the frosting, then place the next cake on top of that one and repeat the process. I like to sprinkle a few chopped walnuts in between each layer. Once you've added the third cake, add the frosting on top and spread the frosting with a flat spatula; if you have a turn table it'll make it easier, but it doesn't have to be perfect. And BEAUTIFUL! You can sprinkle a few more toasted walnuts on top for presentation.

Y LISTO AND ENJOY!

# MINT, PINEAPPLE, AND CUCUMBER POPSICLES

# PALETAS DE PEPINO, PIÑA, Y MENTA

Prep time: 5 minutes,
4 hours with freezing

**MAKES 6 TO 8 POPSICLES**

This is very refreshing and very easy to make—you can also turn it into a cocktail if you add a bit of alcohol! If you're not familiar with them, chamoy is a red, sweet, spicy syrup that is made from either hibiscus or plum; and Tajín is a tangy, dried chile and lime seasoning.

1 cucumber, peeled and chopped

2 cups chopped pineapple

4 sprigs fresh mint

1 tablespoon peeled and diced fresh ginger

Juice of 2 large lemons

1½ cups granulated sugar

### For Serving (optional)

Chamoy

Tajín

### Equipment

8-ounce plastic cups or your favorite popsicle molds

1 • In a blender, add 2 cups of water, the cucumber, pineapple, mint, ginger, and lemon juice and blend until smooth. Strain the mixture into a large bowl and discard any solids. In another large bowl, mix the sugar with 3 cups of water. (I like to mix the sugar in water before adding it into the mixture so that I know all the sugar is dissolved.) Stir into the blended mixture. Taste it, if you'd like you can add more sugar. And BEAUTIFUL!

2 • Divide the mixture among 6 to 8 plastic cups or popsicle molds. Add a wooden popsicle stick and they're ready for the freezer. Freeze for a minimum of 4 hours, until everything is frozen solid, or overnight for the best results. When ready to serve, you can drizzle chamoy and sprinkle some Tajín on them, if desired—the perfect summer popsicles.

**Y LISTO AND ENJOY!**

## EGG NOG POPSICLES

# ROMPOPE BOLIS

Prep time: 5 minutes
plus 4 hours for freezing

**MAKES 8 BOLIS**

4¼ cups whole milk

1 (12-ounce) can
evaporated milk

1 (12-ounce) can
condensed milk

1½ cups Rompope

½ cup powdered milk

1 tablespoon pure vanilla
extract

### Equipment

8 (12 by 2-inch) bolis
bags or regular
popsicle molds

In a blender, add the whole milk, evaporated milk, Rompope, powdered milk, and vanilla and blend well. Divide the mixture among the bolis bags, tie off the tops, and BEAUTIFUL! They are ready for the freezer. Freeze for 4 hours or overnight for best results.

**Y LISTO AND ENJOY!**

These are made in "bolis" bags, which you can buy on Amazon. You pour the mixture in and tie the bag before freezing. Rompope is custardy and milky, essentially eggnog without the alcohol. It's one of the most popular flavors at palaterias in Mexico, which sell only popsicles and bolis. There's no stick involved when you eat a bolis! We wrap napkins around them to prevent frozen fingers. Rompope flavor is also popular with the ice cream man, sold from his cart that goes around the block. Even grownups like it, it tastes a bit like flan. If you don't have bolis bags, you can also use popsicle molds.

# CARAMELIZED CUSTARD

# FLAN DE LECHE

Prep time: 15 minutes
plus 2 hours to set
Cook time: 45 minutes
SERVES 6 TO 8

This is the classic "side dessert"—alongside cake and Jell-O—when we have birthday parties. It's always those three. As a matter of fact, they came out with chocoflan, which is a chocolate cake on the bottom and then a layer of flan on top. I have even seen Jell-O as the final layer! People get so creative. Flan is also part of Thanksgiving or Christmas get-togethers. As standard as tamales for Christmas, it's a celebration recipe.

5 tablespoons granulated sugar

8 large egg yolks

1 (7-ounce) can sweetened condensed milk (La Lechera)

1 (7-ounce) can evaporated milk

2 teaspoons fresh lemon juice

1 teaspoon salt

1 teaspoon pure vanilla extract

## Equipment

1 (8-inch) flan mold

1 • Preheat oven to 375°F.

2 • In the flan mold, melt the sugar over low heat until it turns from clear into an amber, golden-brown color, 6 to 8 minutes. Tilt the mold from side to side to cover the bottom, but do not allow the sugar to burn. Remove from the heat and set aside.

3 • In a medium mixing bowl, gently break and combine the yolks, but do not over mix. Gently stir in the condensed milk and then the evaporated milk until just combined. Stir in the lemon juice, salt, and vanilla. Strain the mixture two to three times through a fine-mesh strainer to eliminate any air bubbles. Next, make one last pass through the strainer directly and slowly into the prepared mold. Cover the mold with aluminum foil. Place the mold in a larger baking dish. Boil water and pour it into the baking dish to surround the mold halfway up the sides with water; you're making a water bath. Be sure to pour the water in after the mold is already in the dish, or else the water may overflow; this is your baño maria. Bake for about 40 minutes, or until firm and a golden crust has formed on top. Allow the mold to cool and then set it in the fridge for 2 hours for best results.

4 • To serve, put a serving plate on top of the mold, lightly tap the top, then quickly flip the whole thing over. It should slide right off!

Y LISTO AND ENJOY!

CARAMELIZED PECANS

# GARAPIÑADO ⊙

Prep time: 5 minutes
Cook time: 15 minutes
MAKES 2½ CUPS

1 cup granulated sugar

2 cups of pecans

2 tablespoons unsalted butter

1 teaspoon salt

I like to make these when I am creating cheese boards. In Mexico, you can buy caramelized pecans on the street in paper cones. As you're passing by the carts selling them the aromas draw you in . . . and you end up buying a pound or two. They're sweet and crunchy and so addicting. Note that you have to manage the heat when cooking because the sugar can burn easily. You must keep stirring or the pecans will stick to the bottom of the pan!

In a medium saucepan, heat ½ cup of water and the sugar over medium heat, and give it a quick stir—I find using a flat, wooden spoon works best. Mix in the pecans, then add the butter, stirring constantly, then stir in the salt. When the water has evaporated, after 6 to 8 minutes, turn off the heat and continue mixing, stirring vigorously so that the pecans don't stick together. When all the pecans are covered in a slightly bubbly and transparent brown sugar liquid, return the saucepan to a low heat and keep mixing. You'll see the sugar at the bottom of the saucepan begin to caramelize and some of the pecans become white with crystalized sugar. Scrape the bottom and mix at the same time until all the pecans have that dry sugary, slightly caramelized look (this is where the word Garapiñadas comes from). BEAUTIFUL! Now, remove from the heat and spread them out onto parchment paper to allow them to cool.

Y LISTO AND ENJOY!

# CANDIED PUMPKIN

# POSTRE DE CALABAZA

**Prep time: 10 minutes**
**Cook time: 1 hour**
**SERVES 10 TO 12**

1 large (8-pound) pumpkin (calabaza de cascara dura)

2 cinnamon sticks, broken in half

2 piloncillo cones (Mexican brown sugar cones)

3 whole cloves

4 tablespoons light brown sugar

2 teaspoons freshly ground nutmeg

Milk, for serving

Candied pumpkin is big in Mexico, especially in Michoacan where my mother is from. During pumpkin season, we make big pots of this. The type of pumpkin that we use, calabaza de castilla or calabaza de cascara dura, has a very hard, thick skin, so it doesn't get too soft when you cook it. I've seen others make a similar recipe but with more spices. My mom keeps it simple. She'll also use this method for sweet potatoes, and those leftovers always end up in a pie or empanadas.

Start by scooping out the seeds and stringy membrane, then slice the pumpkin into wedges. I follow the lines of the pumpkin. Then, to a large, tall pot over medium heat, combine 6 cups of water, the cinnamon, piloncillos, and cloves; stir until the piloncillos have dissolved. Add the pumpkin to the pot, but make sure you place the slices with the skin facing down. Baste the pumpkin until the slices are coated. Sprinkle the brown sugar and nutmeg on top. Cover and cook until soft, about 1 hour. BEAUTIFUL! The way we eat it in Michoacan is served in a small bowl with about a cup of milk poured on top.

**Y LISTO AND ENJOY!**

## MEXICAN BREAD PUDDING

# CAPIROTADA ESTILO MICHOACAN

Prep time: 10 minutes
Cook time: 40 minutes
SERVES 8 TO 10

This is my mom's famous dessert that the whole the family asks her to make during lent. It's commonly served to celebrate Good Friday, but she makes it every Friday during lent because we like it so much! Think of it as the Mexican version of bread pudding. You mix everything in, like a big mess of food, and use day-old, dried bread. In Mexican groceries, you can buy bags of capirotada bread that is pre-dried. They cut it into large croutons and sell it mainly for use in this dish. Throwing food away is a sin, after all. We always recycle food. To rehydrate and flavor this dried bread they came up with a syrup. There are many versions, but this is the Michoacan style. Some people add candy, shredded coconut, or nuts. But my mom always says, the simpler the better, you enjoy it more. And it's true less is more; she's right when it comes to this dessert. We use queso fresco, tomato, whole cloves, and peppercorns—and you might get thrown off by the onion! But you'd never imagine all of that was in there, you really can't taste it, as it all melds into a really sweet syrup.

8 small (5-inch) Mexican bolillos, day-old or longer

½ cup pork lard (manteca)

1 cup black raisins

1 Roma tomato, sliced

¼ white onion

4 piloncillo cones (Mexican brown sugar cones)

1 cinnamon stick

3 whole cloves

3 whole black peppercorns

4 to 6 (6-inch) corn tortillas

16 ounces queso fresco

1 • Begin by cutting the bolillo into 2-inch slices. In a frying pan, heat the lard over medium-low heat, and fry the bread slices until they are golden brown, about 2 minutes on each side. Drain on a cooling rack and set aside.

2 • Meanwhile, in a medium saucepan, bring to a boil over medium heat 8 cups of water, the raisins, tomato, onion, piloncillos, cinnamon, cloves, and peppercorns. Reduce the heat to medium-low and simmer until the mixture thickens slightly, 15 to 20 minutes.

3 • To begin the base, dip 4 to 6 tortillas in the sweet liquid and place them flat in a large pot, such as a Dutch oven, until the entire bottom of the pot is covered. This will prevent the bread from sticking to the bottom of the pot as it cooks. Next, dip and soak each bread slice in the sweet liquid for 20 to 30 seconds, then remove and begin layering them in the pot. Between every layer of bread sprinkle a few raisins that have been removed from the syrup, sprinkle with some queso fresco, and drizzle a little of the syrup over the top. Repeat the layering process until all the bread is in the pot. Cover and simmer over low heat until warmed, for 5 to 8 minutes. Serve each person 2 to 3 pieces of the bread.

Y LISTO AND ENJOY!

SWEET BREAD

# CONCHAS

Prep time: 2 hours 45 minutes
Cook time: 20 minutes

**MAKES 12 CONCHAS**

This is the sweet Mexican bread that's found in every home. It's a classic comfort food, and what the elderly always purchase. Have it with coffee for breakfast or after dinner.

## For the Batter

2¼ teaspoons (1 package) active dry yeast

¾ cup milk, warmed

½ cup granulated sugar, divided

½ 1 stick (8 tablespoons) unsalted butter, melted

3 large eggs, at room temperature

1 teaspoon pure vanilla extract

4½ cups all-purpose flour, divided

1 teaspoon salt

## For the Sweet Dough Topping

1 cup all-purpose flour

1 cup confectioners' sugar

1 stick (8 tablespoons) unsalted butter, softened

1 tablespoon pure vanilla extract

1 • Start by combining the yeast and warm water with ¼ cup of sugar in a stand mixer bowl. Lightly mix, and set aside until the yeast has formed a foamy top layer, about 5 minutes. Add the butter, the remaining ¼ cup sugar, the eggs, and vanilla, then whisk until well combined. In a separate bowl, mix the flour and salt. Add 2 cups of flour to the yeast mixture and whisk by hand to create a batter. Place the bowl in the stand mixer and, using the dough hook, add the remaining flour in small increments, kneading until the dough is smooth and well combined, about 10 minutes. You will know the dough is ready when you press your finger into the dough and it does not stick to your finger. Transfer the dough to a greased bowl and let is rise until doubled in size, about 2 hours in a warm spot. It can take longer during cold weather.

2 • **FOR THE SWEET DOUGH TOPPING:** Mix the flour and confectioners' sugar in a bowl, then add the butter and vanilla. Combine with your hands until you get a sugar dough–like consistency. (Note: If you would like to make different color toppings, this is when to divide the sugar dough and mix in the food coloring.) Set aside.

(recipe continues on page 200)

3 • Preheat the oven to 350°F. Line a baking sheet with parchment paper and set aside.

4 • Place the risen dough on a floured surface and divide it into 12 dough balls. Roll each dough ball into a round concha shape by pinching it together. You will have a rough side and a smooth, pretty side. Use your thumb and middle finger to make a small circle and gently roll it out into the shape. Place each dough ball on the prepared baking sheet.

5 • For each concha, take 1 tablespoon of the sweet dough topping and roll it out with a rolling pin into a thin circle, about the size of the concha. Drape over the concha ball. With a knife, carefully score the sweet dough topping to create a concha pattern. Loosely cover with plastic wrap and set the dough aside for about 30 minutes, or until the dough doubles in size.

6 • Once doubled, bake for about 20 minutes, or until lightly golden brown.

**Y LISTO AND ENJOY!**

## THREE KINGS BREAD

# ROSCA DE REYES

Prep time: 2 hours 15 minutes
Cook time: 35 minutes
SERVES 10 TO 12

4 cups all-purpose flour

¾ cup granulated sugar

2¼ teaspoons (1 pack) active dry yeast

1 teaspoon salt

4 large eggs

1 tablespoon orange zest

1 teaspoon pure vanilla extract

1 cup milk, warmed

1 stick (8 tablespoons) unsalted butter, at room temperature

1 Mexican cinnamon stick, finely crushed

4 ounces membrillo (quince paste), cut into 5 by ½-inch strips

4 ounces guava paste, cut into 5 by ½-inch

### For the Dough Topping

1 cup confectioners' sugar

1 cup all-purpose flour

1 stick (8 tablespoons) unsalted butter, softened

¾ ounce dark chocolate (I like to use Abuelita chocolate)

Cajeta (milk caramel sauce), for serving

This recipe is like a large Concha. If you leave it in the oven longer than it should be, the candy and sugar on top can burn, so you have to keep an eye on this one. We have this on January 6, as it's the day of the three wise men or kings. My sister Reyna was born on that day, so we would all gather at her house and every year we would have a rosca de reyes. There's a tradition to hide a "baby Jesus" inside the bread, and nobody knows who will get it in their slice. And it's a game, because whoever gets the baby Jesus has to make the tamales on February 2, the day of Candelaria. So everybody tries to avoid getting it! I usually buy Cajeta at the Mexican grocery store, or you can find it on Amazon.

1 • Start by mounding the flour on a clean, flat surface, and add the sugar, yeast, and salt. Mix and create a well in the center. To the well, add the eggs, orange zest, and vanilla, and whisk the egg mixture, initially without incorporating the flour. Gradually whisk in the milk. Bit by bit, mix the flour into the center of the well and incorporate it into the wet ingredients. Add the butter and combine everything by hand until it forms a dough-like consistency. Add the dough to the bowl of a stand mixer and knead for 5 minutes using the dough hook attachment, or knead by hand until smooth, about 15 minutes. Place in a greased bowl, cover, and let the dough rise until doubled in size, 1 to 2 hours.

2 • Prepare a baking sheet lined with parchment paper. Punch the dough down, and on a clean surface, roll it out into a square-like shape. Sprinkle the crushed cinnamon all over the dough. Start rolling it into a long log, about 24 to 30 inches long. Connect the ends to form a circle and to achieve the rosca-style shape. Place it on the prepared baking sheet and set aside.

3 • For the sugar dough topping, in a large bowl, mix the confectioners' sugar, flour, and butter until you get a dough-like consistency. Cut the sugar topping dough in half and cover with plastic wrap. Chill in the refrigerator for 5 minutes. In a small saucepan over low heat, melt the chocolate Abuelita. Mix it into the remaining half of the sugar topping doughs in order to have two different flavors/colors. Roll both sugar doughs out thinly, and cut into 5 by ½-inch strips. Lay the strips over the rosca dough, alternating with

membrillo and guava paste, to create colorful stripes. Let sit for 1 hour.

4 • Preheat the oven to 375°F.

5 • After the dough has sat for 1 hour, bake for about 30 minutes or until golden brown. Drizzle cajeta over the top.

**Y LISTO AND ENJOY!**

# BUÑUELOS

Prep time: 10 minutes
Cook time: 50 to 70 minutes
**MAKES ABOUT 24 BUÑUELOS**

These go viral when people make them, my video included. Served during the holidays, they taste like crispy churros. Each mold has its own unique form, but all are circular snowflake shapes. This recipe was introduced to me by my husband's sister-in-law, Adriana. I thought they looked intimidating to make, but they're not complicated, they just burn easily! If you have a new buñuelo mold, you have to treat it a bit like a cast-iron pan; it needs to be cured. Let it sit in the hot oil for at least ten minutes, then remove it to a paper towel to cool down a bit. Then place it back into the hot oil to get it a little hot. After that you can add it to the batter but never allow the batter to go over the edge of the mold. The batter sticks to and coats the hot mold, then you quickly put it in the oil to fry it. As it hardens and fries, you shake it gently to help it release. When the buñuelo turns golden brown it releases on its own and you remove the buñuelo quickly from the oil.

Making buñuelos takes some technique, but they're worth it in the end. It does take time because you have to do them one at a time. To make this all go faster, I recommend buying more than one mold; once you are comfortable, you can work up to having three going at the same time!

(recipe continues on page 205)

## For the Batter

2 cups all-purpose flour

1 teaspoon baking powder

¼ teaspoon salt

1½ cups milk, at room temperature

2 large eggs, at room temperature

2 tablespoons granulated sugar

1 teaspoon pure vanilla extract

4¼ cups canola oil, divided

## For the Cinnamon Sugar Topping

1 teaspoon ground cinnamon

⅓ cup granulated sugar

1 • In a large bowl, mix the flour, baking powder, and salt. In a separate medium bowl, whisk the milk and eggs, add the sugar and vanilla, and whisk again. Add the wet mixture to the dry mixture and mix to create the batter. Set aside.

2 • Pour 4 cups of toil into a deep pan over medium heat. Check the heat by dipping a wooden spoon into the hot oil; if it sizzles, it's ready.

3 • While the oil heats up, make the topping: In a shallow bowl, mix the cinnamon and sugar and set aside.

4 • In a small saucepan over medium heat, add the remaining ¼ cup of oil to keep the buñuelo mold hot in between each buñuelo. Once the buñuelo mold has been sitting in the oil for about 1 minute, pat the oil off with a paper towel. Dip the hot mold into the batter enough to cover the entire mold without going over the top edges of the mold. Immediately place into the 4 cups oil; when the fried dough starts separating from the mold, after about 1 minute, begin to carefully shake the mold in order to help the buñuelo to release from the mold. Cook until golden brown, about 2 minutes each side. Watch carefully as they can easily burn. Drain on a cooling rack and transfer to the cinnamon sugar mixture to coat both sides. Repeat the process for each buñuelo. Serve on a platter.

**Y LISTO AND ENJOY!**

2 sticks (16 tablespoons) unsalted butter, softened

2 cups confectioners' sugar, divided

1 teaspoon pure vanilla extract

2 cups all-purpose flour

1 cup raw pecans, finely chopped

# POLVORONES

Prep time: 25 minutes
Cook time: 12 minutes
MAKES ABOUT 2 DOZEN

These are called snowballs in English. You won't want to stop eating them. We make them every year around the holidays, and the kids love them. They leave their powdered-sugar fingerprints everywhere around the house. Really nice to see them enjoying these.

1 • Preheat the oven to 350°F. Line a baking sheet with parchment paper.

2 • In a large bowl, cream the butter with 1 cup of sugar and the vanilla until smooth. Gradually add the flour. Fold in the chopped pecans. Using a cookie scoop if you have one, scoop out about 1 tablespoon of the cookie dough. Place the dough balls about 1 inch apart on the prepared baking sheet.

3 • Bake for about 12 minutes, or until the edges are golden brown. Allow the cookies to cool for about 15 minutes. Place the remaining cup of sugar into a bowl and fully coat each cookie, one at a time.

**Y LISTO AND ENJOY!**

# DRINKS

Pineapple Margarita

✦

Irish Mule with a Twist

✦

Pomegranate Margarita

✦

Cantarito

✦

La Perfecta Toxica
(PERFECT TOXIC MARGARITA)

✦

Agua de Pepino con Limon
(CUCUMBER LIMEADE)

✦

Agua de Sandia
(WATERMELON WATER)

✦

# PINEAPPLE MARGARITA

Prep time: 5 minutes

SERVES 1

1½ cups diced fresh pineapple, divided

1 fresh lime wedge

1 ounce orange triple sec

2 ounces silver tequila

2 tablespoons Tajín, for garnish

Slice of pineapple, for garnish

I fell in love with the pineapple margarita after I tried one in a restaurant; there's something about the pairing. I was so used to lime, pomegranate, or watermelon, but after I tried this I told my son, who is my personal mixologist, you better nail this one! It's the fresh pineapple that makes a huge difference when you blend these flavors. And the juice of that pineapple is so sweet it creates a natural simple syrup. I have so many favorite cocktails but this is one of the top ones.

1 • In a cocktail shaker, muddle well 1 cup of pinapple. Squeeze the lime into the shaker but save the used lime wedge for later. Add the triple sec and tequila and set aside.

2 • Now prepare the glass. Put about 2 tablespoons of the Tajín on a flat plate. With the used lime wedge, rub the rim of the glass to wet it and flip it over onto the plate so that the Tajín coats the rim. Add ice to the glass and top it off with the remaining ½ cup of pineapple.

3 • Grab the cocktail shaker and shake well; you want to shake this until you get that froth on top! Pour through the strainer into the prepared glass and BEAUTIFUL! Dab the slice of pineapple into the remaining Tajín and lay over the top of the glass as a garnish.

Y LISTO AND ENJOY!

# IRISH MULE WITH A TWIST

Prep time: 5 minutes

SERVES 1

5 fresh mint leaves, plus more for garnish

6 ounces ginger beer

2 ounces Jameson® whiskey

Juice of ¼ fresh lime

2 scoops Mexican lime sorbet (called nieve garrafa in Mexico)

First place the mint into your cocktail shaker so that it will immediately begin to infuse with the wet ingredients. Then add the ginger beer, Jameson, and the lime juice and stir well. (You don't want to shake this because the of the ginger beer.) Pour into a copper cup, as these are perfect for mules. Add 1 scoop Mexican lime sorbet and give it a quick mix. Add ice, and top it off with the remaining 1 scoop of Mexican lime sorbet and garnish with mint.

**Y LISTO AND ENJOY!**

We've tried the Moscow mule, but this version is my husband's favorite. Instead of a sweetener, we use Mexican lime sorbet. You can even use a lime popsicle. My cousin Erika can do anything, and she makes lime ice cream sweetened with brown sugar, all by hand, churned in a barrel full of ice. She mixes until it's creamy and icy and sells it in front of the schools in Mexico. Inspired by those flavors, I told my son, the mixologist, to try it in the Irish Mule, and it's our special twist!

# POMEGRANATE MARGARITA

Prep time: 5 minutes

SERVES 1

4 ounces freshly
squeezed pomegranate
juice

1 ounce silver tequila

1 ounce orange triple sec

Juice of ½ lime

Tajín, for garnish

Pomegranate chunk, for
garnish

I love pomegranate by itself, so I'm happy mixing it with tequila or even in a pomegranate martini. We have lived in this house for over twenty years, and about ten houses down there is the best pomegranate tree. My kids go on their bikes, literally around the corner, and they grab two big, heavy bags full. The owner tells them to take them all, and they do! They are so high in antioxidants; I am getting my tequila and antioxidants at the same time. To your health!

To a cocktail shaker, add the pomegranate juice, tequila, triple sec, and lime juice. Shake well but be careful because pomegranate juice stains. Set aside and prepare a glass. With the used lime, rub the rim of the glass to wet it and flip it over onto the plate so that the Tajín coats the rim. Add ice and pour in the pomegranate margarita. BEAUTIFUL! Now break off a chunk of pomegranate and garnish the glass.

**Y LISTO AND ENJOY!**

# CANTARITO

Prep time: 5 minutes
SERVES 1

3 ounces Squirt®
  (grapefruit-lime soda,
  like Fresca)

2 ounces silver tequila

1 ounce grapefruit juice

1 ounce orange juice

Juice of ½ lime

1 teaspoon rock salt

Garnish

Tajín

Chamoy

Lime slices

Orange slices

Equipment

Cantarito

A cantarito is the famous clay mug with no handle, made from raw clay with no glaze. You'll want to have these for this drink as it actually makes a huge difference in the taste! It automatically takes people back to Mexico. Many homes in Mexico are made from adobe, and my mom loves to talk about the smell of the walls and the pounded dirt floors that she would wet a bit each morning so the dust would not go into the air. It's beautiful, you can smell that earth in the clay from the cup. You must keep these mugs hydrated or you'll find they soak up half your drink! Keep them underwater until just before you pour the drink as the clay dries out quickly.

It's become trendy to serve these in LA, bartenders have bowls of the mugs in water. Or you can find them on the streets in Mexico or at the festivals. Just make sure it is served in a real clay mug. It doesn't tase the same otherwise, almost like cooking on a seasoned cast-iron or grinding on a molcajete, the difference in the flavor is unexplainable.

In a cocktail shaker, combine the Squirt, tequila, grapefruit juice, orange juice, lime juice, and salt. Stir well. Now prepare a cantarito (clay mug). Put about 2 tablespoons of Tajín on a flat plate. Rub the rim of the mug with chamoy to wet it and then flip it over onto the plate so that the Tajín coats the rim. Add 1 cup of ice and pour the drink into the cantarito. BEAUTIFUL! Garnish with a lime slice and an orange slice.

**Y LISTO AND ENJOY!**

PERFECT TOXIC MARGARITA

# LA PERFECTA TOXICA

Prep time: 5 minutes

SERVES 1

3 dried chiles de árbol, stemmed

1½ tablespoons Tajín

½ cup plus 2 tablespoons store-bought, bottled margarita mix

2 ounces tequila reposado

1 ounces orange triple sec

½ ounce orange juice

Juice of ½ fresh lime

1 dried chile de árbol, for garnish

### Equipment

Molcajete

For all the crazy followers I have, this is a drink that is SPICY. I have infused tequilas with jalapeños in the past, but with this one, you don't have to wait for the chile to infuse; the chile is ground up and you're tasting it as you drink! We got creative adding a twist to my son's perfect margarita. We first discovered the perfect margarita at a restaurant in Ensenada, so we played with the ingredients, and wanted to spice it up. Toxica means it's so extra. When you're drunk, you're not bothered by the heat, as it blends so well with the tequila. The spice is in the mix and on the rim. And it's like a volcano in your tummy. Caution: When you go to the rest room you will feel it . . .

Grind the chiles in the molcajete until they start turning into a powder. Add the Tajín and continue grinding, just enough to mix well. Set aside. (Note that you will have extra for future use.) To a shaker, add the margarita mix, tequila, triple sec, orange juice, lime juice, and 1 teaspoon of the chili powder mixture. Add ice and shake well until you get that froth. Grab a rock glass, rim it with lime juice then the chili powder mixture, add 1 cup of ice, and pour the margarita into the cup. And BEAUTIFUL! Sprinkle some chili powder mixture on top of the froth and garnish it with a chile de árbol.

Y LISTO AND ENJOY!

CUCUMBER LIMEADE

# AGUA DE PEPINO CON LIMON

**Prep time: 5 minutes**

**MAKES 1 GALLON**

**4 cups granulated sugar, divided**

**3 cucumbers (pepinos), roughly chopped, plus slices for garnish**

**Juice of 3 fresh limes**

**1** • Add 3½ quarts of water to your favorite punch bowl, then add 3 cups of sugar and stir until the sugar has dissolved.

**2** • In a blender, add the cucumber along with 2 cups of water, the remaining 1 cup of sugar, and the lime juice. Blend until smooth. If you don't have a high-powered blender, make sure you strain your cucumber juice. Now stir the mixture into the punch bowl and BEAUTIFUL! Garnish with a few slices of cucumber and taste for sweetness; you can add more sugar if you prefer.

**Y LISTO AND ENJOY!**

If my dad sees a seed, he sees life. He puts them in his pockets when he eats, and he already knows where he wants to plant them. A couple weeks later you see a little green plant. There are so many different citrus types, and he knows exactly where he planted them. My brothers and sisters and I all have so many citrus trees growing in our yards thanks to him! I am now blessed with ten lemon trees in my backyard, so I never have to go buy any. He comes and takes some for my siblings, and I say sure, they're your trees!

Here we use lime and add cucumber; it's a true refresher. And if you want a cucumber margarita, boom there you go!

WATERMELON WATER

# AGUA DE SANDIA

**Prep time: 5 minutes**
**MAKES 1 GALLON**

4 cups granulated sugar, divided

3 cups chopped watermelon

Juice of 2 fresh lemons

**1** • Add 3½ quarts of water to your favorite punch bowl, then add 3 cups of sugar and stir until the sugar is dissolved.

**2** • In a blender, add the watermelon, 2 cups of water, the remaining 1 cup of sugar, and the lemon juice and blend well. If you don't have a high-powered blender, make sure you strain your watermelon juice. Now stir the mixture into the punch bowl and BEAUTIFUL! Taste for sweetness; you can add more sugar if you prefer (you can also rim your cup with chamoy and Tajín!).

**Y LISTO AND ENJOY!**

My kids always want watermelon, and I notice most of my TikTok fans go crazy for watermelon. If I make candy-based watermelon or a chamoy, or even if I just cut it on camera, it grabs their attention. Perhaps it's the beautiful colors? I feel better giving this rather than soda to the kids, and its healthier than many juices as you can control the amount of sugar.

It's great in summertime and you can play with the combinations. You can even mix it with flax or chia seeds.

# ✦ ✦ ✦

# ACKNOWLEDGMENTS

It's been a dream of mine to honor my mom in some way, and I am so proud that this cookbook showcases so many of her recipes. The passion she had for cooking for her family—and teaching her children her recipes—is now my passion. I wrote this cookbook holding the same joy that she held every day in her kitchen, at every meal. I want to thank my fans and followers from all my social media platforms for making this dream happen. I appreciate you and thank you, from the bottom of my heart, for all the love I get on the daily.

I literally live in my kitchen, cooking and reinventing, creating shortcuts as I cook for my family, but keeping the traditional, authentic ways. I do it all with the help of my husband, Arnie, and my children: Anthony, Cindy, Evan, and Josh. They are my biggest cheerleaders but also critics when it comes to my food. They can be brutally honest if it's good or not, but I appreciate that they tell me the truth so that I can perfect the recipes.

Thank you to my father, who has been such a loving parent and a wonderful husband to my mother. He is a great example to follow and has been there for all his children, no matter what. Thank you for planting all my fruit trees and giving life to my back yard and for always having a smile and being willing to help. Mami gracias por todo su amor y cariño y por siempre valorando y apoyando mis sueños y ideas junto con todas mis locuras! Los amo a los dos con todas mis fuerzas.

Thank you to my husband, Arnulfo, who has supported all my dreams, not only helping around the house but with the children when they were little so that I could continue working on my career. He has always made me believe that I can do whatever I want to by putting God first and following His timing, lifting me up with positive words and prayers. There are no excuses to make for what you do in life, as long as you have the courage and discipline to work hard and pursue your dream, and the people around you will see it, too!

To all my children, especially the oldest ones for leaving good jobs in order to support me with their talents. Thank you for seeing how passionate I get and helping me turn this social media craziness into our family business. I wouldn't have made it without you guys!

To my good friend and great chef Rocco DiSpirito. How did I get so incredibly lucky to work with you? I'm thankful for the day that our lives crossed paths. Your guidance and advice gave me so much confidence in the culinary world, and I will be forever grateful!

I couldn't believe when a publisher reached out to me! I cried of joy as this was finally a way to give back to my mom for everything that she's down for us! Huge thanks to the publishing team at Simon Element and Simon and Schuster, my agent, Andrea Barzvi, my co-author, Ann Volkwein, photographer Jennifer Chong, and food stylist Laura Kinsey Dolph.

And special thanks to my editor, Justin Schwartz, for believing in me and taking the time in working closely with me to create this beautiful book!!

# INDEX

# S